ABOUT THE AUTHORS

Richard B. Bliss, Ed.D., has more than 39 years experience in all areas of science education. In Addition to having taught chemistry, physics, biology, and general science at the high school level, he was adjunct professor, teaching science methods to teachers in the University of Wisconsin System. He was engaged in biological research and obtained several National Science Foundation grants and fellowships during his academic career. Recently he developed a hands-on curriculum in science for K-6 elementary students that is based on the most current research in science education. Dr. Bliss is a frequent speaker on the creation/evolution issue in the U.S. and other countries. He is presently professor of science education and Chairman of the Science Education Department at the Institute for Creation Research in Santee, California.

Gary E. Parker, Ed.D., formerly ICR Research Associate and Professor of Biology, is now Head of Natural Sciences at Clearwater Christian College, Clearwater, Florida. He did his doctoral work in biology (amphibian endocrinology) and geology and is the author of five widely used program instruction books in biology, including *Life's Basis: Biomolecules* (Wiley), and *DNA: The Key to Life* (Educational Methods). Dr. Parker, a member of Phi Beta Kappa, has received several competitive scholarships, including an award from the National Science Foundation.

Duane T. Gish, Ph.D., is Vice President of the Institute for Creation Research in California. He spent 18 years in biochemical research at Cornell University Medical College, the Virus Laboratory of the University of California, Berkeley, and The Upjohn Company, Kalamazoo, Michigan. He is the author and co-author of numerous technical articles in his field and is a well-known author and lecturer on creation/evolution. He received his Ph.D. in biochemistry from the University of California, Berkeley.

ACKNOWLEDGMENT

The printing of this publication was made possible through the generous participation of Mr. and Mrs. V. Keith Bestor of LaMirada, California.

CONTENTS

FOSSILS:

KEY TO THE PRESENT

EVOLUTION • CREATION

RICHARD B. BLISS, Ed.D.

Director of Curriculum Development
Institute for Creation Research

GARY E. PARKER, Ed.D.

Head of Natural Sciences
Clearwater Christian College

DUANE T. GISH, Ph.D.

Vice President
Institute for Creation Research

C·L·P PUBLISHERS

San Diego, California

FOSSILS: Key to the Present

First Edition   1980
  Third Printing   1990

Copyright © 1980
C·L·P· PUBLISHERS
P.O. Box 1606
El Cajon, CA 92021

Library of Congress Catalog Card Number 79-53426
ISBN 0-89051-058-X

Cataloging in Publication Data
Bliss, Richard Burt, 1923-
  Fossils: key to the present
  1. Paleontology.   I. Parker, Gary E. 1940-
II. Gish, Duane T. 1921   III. Title
                          560   79-53426
ISBN 0-89051-058-X

Printed in the United States of America

Groups of fossils found in different parts of the world can be put together in an arrangement called the geologic column. What can these fossils tell us about the origin and history of life on earth?

INTRODUCTION

To the Student

Did all life that we see today form very slowly over vast periods of time? Was there a time when a Creator, a Master Designer, created all the different kinds of life on earth? Neither of these questions can be answered with certainty. It has been said by some that the study of fossils provides a means of "seeing **evolution**." Others have stated that the fossil evidence favors "**creation**." Perhaps the student can decide, by observing the **data**, which idea seems to fit best.

Yes, a "**two-model**" study of this question is a way to approach the data through "**scientific inquiry**." If you have an opportunity to study all of the data, you can decide which model makes more sense to you. Evolution and creation are both models that are opposites in many ways. The actual scientific data, however, can be explained in both models. We will try to bring these data to you in a very **objective way**. Which of these two you decide upon is up to you.

A study made in 1978 showed that students, like you, learn more about the facts of origins when they study from two models. The study showed that students strengthened their critical thought habits this way. In fact, these students seemed to be more objective than those taught only evolution.

The very purpose of this module is to lead you to the scientific data and some of the arguments from science. The final decision, however, is yours to make. This module will help you to think critically, and through this, your decision-making skills will be strengthened.

The authors

evolution: *(ev-o-'loo-shun)* the idea that offspring of simple life forms can change into varied and more complex kinds over long periods of time; change *between* kinds

creation: *(cree-'a-shun)* the idea that all life forms are varieties of kinds created by a Master Designer; change *within* kinds

data: facts based on observation; information used to compare ideas, such as evolution and creation

two-model: comparing two points of view on a subject, both to encourage careful thinking and to avoid prejudice

scientific inquiry: using logic and observation in an orderly approach to solving problems

objective way: using fair judgment and not permitting bias to cloud the mind

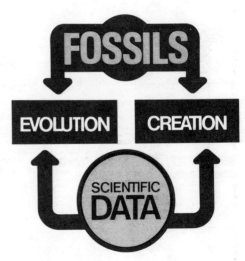

MAJOR GEOLOGIC SYSTEMS

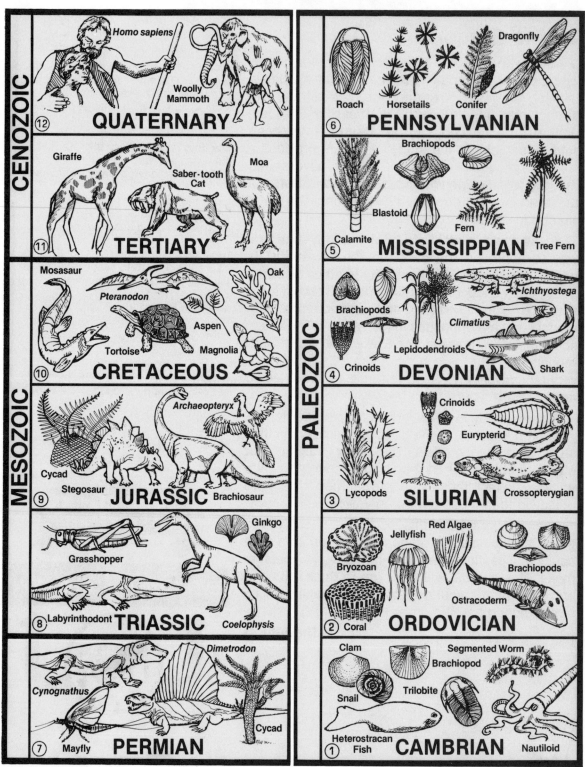

CENOZOIC

⑫ QUATERNARY — Homo sapiens, Woolly Mammoth

⑪ TERTIARY — Giraffe, Saber-tooth Cat, Moa

MESOZOIC

⑩ CRETACEOUS — Mosasaur, Pteranodon, Tortoise, Aspen, Magnolia, Oak

⑨ JURASSIC — Cycad, Stegosaur, Archaeopteryx, Brachiosaur

⑧ TRIASSIC — Grasshopper, Ginkgo, Labyrinthodont, Coelophysis

⑦ PERMIAN — Cynognathus, Dimetrodon, Mayfly, Cycad

PALEOZOIC

⑥ PENNSYLVANIAN — Roach, Horsetails, Conifer, Dragonfly

⑤ MISSISSIPPIAN — Brachiopods, Blastoid, Fern, Tree Fern, Calamite

④ DEVONIAN — Brachiopods, Crinoids, Lepidodendroids, Climatius, Ichthyostega, Shark

③ SILURIAN — Lycopods, Crinoids, Eurypterid, Crossopterygian

② ORDOVICIAN — Bryozoan, Jellyfish, Red Algae, Brachiopods, Coral, Ostracoderm

① CAMBRIAN — Clam, Snail, Segmented Worm, Brachiopod, Trilobite, Heterostracan Fish, Nautiloid

2

CHAPTER ONE

FOSSILS: Clues to the Past

What was the earth like when dinosaurs roamed over the world? Has anyone ever seen a living dinosaur? Why do we find sea creatures preserved in stone high up on mountains all over the world? These questions, and those relating to the origin of life, are important to the student today. Was all life created by a **supernatural** Master Designer? Is all life the result of chance and evolutionary **selection**?

Fossils can help us compare the evolution and creation models. The very fact that fossils are found today helps us understand some of the past. In spite of this, questions are not easy to answer from existing evidence. We have no detailed scientific records of life's beginnings. There were no human **eyewitnesses**. We only have clues about what life was like in the past. The fossils provide these for us, for they help us to look into the past. If you like mysteries, you will enjoy solving the fossil puzzle. You even may want to join the many rock and fossil hunters called **"rock hounds."** Professional fossil scientists are called paleontologists.

supernatural: beyond the natural; something that one could not normally expect to happen

selection: survival in greater numbers of varieties that fit best into their environment

eyewitness: someone having been on the spot to see something happen

rock hounds: people around the world who enjoy searching for rocks and fossils—they often form clubs

What Are Fossils?

Fossils are the remains or traces of plants and animals **preserved** in rock deposits. At Dinosaur National Monument in Utah (Figure 1.1), you can see fossil remains of dinosaurs in the rocks. You can even watch scientists, called paleontologists (pay-le-on-'tol-o-gists) dig out these bones. They take their finds to the museum to rebuild a whole skeleton.

preserved: kept at least partly in their original form after death

Figure 1.1 *Extracting fossils from the surrounding rock is a very slow process. This scientist is taking extreme care so that he can be sure every particle of the fossil is intact.*

Maybe you have found fossils yourself. They are often common where streams or roads cut through **sedimentary** rocks. *Sedimentary* rocks, as the name suggests, are formed from **sediments**. Sandstone, limestone, and shale are examples of *sedimentary* rocks (Figure 1.2).

sedimentary: *(sed-i-'ment-'ah-ree)* rocks formed from materials dropped or deposited by water or wind, such as sandstone, limestone, or shale (Figure 1.2)

sediments: materials, like sand, lime, mud, or clay, that settle out of water; they can turn into sedimentary rocks

One of the authors (Gary Parker) has collected over 500 kg. (1,100 lbs.) of fossils from road cuts and streambeds all over North America. Some of these fossils are shown in Figure 1.3.

petrified: when minerals dissolved in ground water replace the cells of a dead tree or bone, and produce a "mineral copy" of the organism

Most fossils look like creatures that are living today: clams, snails, sea stars, sea lilies (crinoids), shark teeth (even from Sioux City, Iowa!), and bits of **petrified** wood from pine trees and many others.

Some fossils show **extinct** forms of life, those no longer living today. Dinosaurs are *extinct* and so are most of the different kinds of **lampshells** (brachiopods) (Figure 1.4). The famous fossils called **trilobites** (Figure 1.4) are *extinct* sea animals. They looked something like horseshoe crabs.

extinct: found only as a fossil; not found alive today

lampshells: common name for brachiopods, animals with arms of tentacles living inside top and bottom shells (Figure 1.4)

trilobites: extinct animals with three body lobes, jointed legs, a crab-like outer skeleton, and sometimes eyes (Figure 1.4)

Figure 1.2 *Sedimentary rock is formed from sediments that have cementing agents in them. The chemicals in the sediments influence the rapidity of rock formation, and these and other factors influence the hardness.*

Figure 1.3 *Fossils like these include some kinds of organisms that are still living and others that are extinct.*

Figure 1.4 *Can you recognize the three body sections and large eyes of the trilobites shown? The lampshells (brachiopods) have two shells like clams, but the animal is quite different and the shells are usually unequal, unlike clams.*

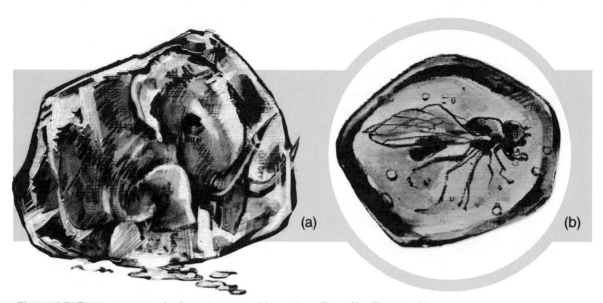

(a)

(b)

Figure 1.5 *Frozen mammoths have been found with their flesh intact (a). What kind of catastrophe caused this is uncertain. Insects have been found perfectly preserved in amber in many locations throughout the world (b). Can you imagine how this entrapment occurred?*

water-borne sediment: sediment that has been transported by water, rather than wind, etc.

Figure 1.6 *Typical fossilization can occur when the organism is (a) trapped, (b) buried, and (c) the general outlines or parts are preserved in the rock.*

How Are Fossils Formed?

Wooly mammoths are found trapped in ice, and insects may be *preserved* in pine resin that hardened into amber (Figure 1.5), but such fossils are rare exceptions to the general rule.

Most often, the fossil-making process starts when a plant or animal gets buried. This often occurs under a heavy load of **water-borne sediment,** such as mud or sand. The load of *sediment* kills the creature and keeps its remains together. Often, however, the soft parts will rot away, and only hard parts like teeth, bones, shells, and wood get *preserved.*

Most scientists agree that flooding provides the best way to start forming fossils. A flood usually comes without warning, so many animals cannot

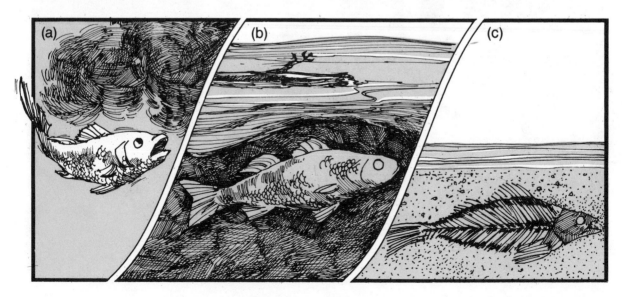

(a)

(b)

(c)

escape. A flood also carries enough *sediment* to bury living things deeply enough so that they cannot crawl out. Some **fossil graveyards** include remains of thousands, even billions, of these forms of life all washed together under the same *sediment* load. The way fossils usually form is shown in Figures 1.6, 1.7a, and 1.7b.

As the *sediment* that traps this life turns into rock, parts of the once-living plants and animals usually become like rock. They absorb minerals and we say they have become *petrified.* Ordinarily, when clams die they decay with no remains, while a clam becoming a rock-like fossil can keep its shape.

Sometimes, instead of getting harder and heavier, though, a bone has its minerals **leached** or washed away. Leaching leaves the bone very light and fragile. The huge, but lightweight, mammoth bone in Figure 1.7b can easily be held with the fingers.

fossil graveyards: large groups of fossils that look as if they all died together or were washed into the same burial site (p.73)

leached: washed away, as when water passes through a fossil and takes part of the material away

Figure 1.7a Sometimes clams are found with body parts and shells completely hardened. Most often they decay and leave no remains. When woody tissue hardens, it is said to be petrified. This can only occur when minerals are present to replace living cells.

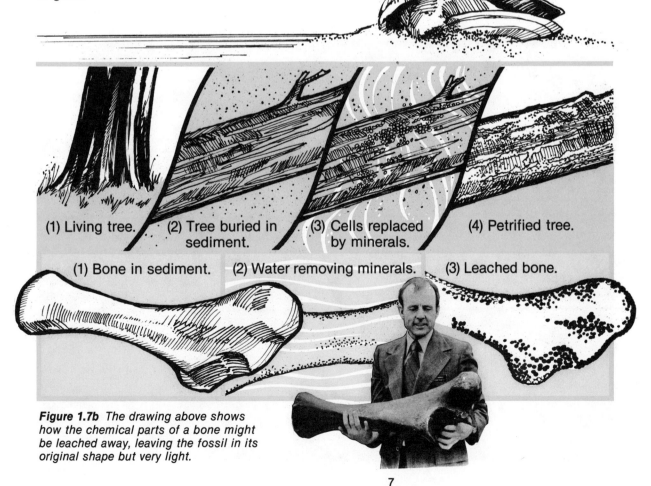

(1) Living tree.   (2) Tree buried in sediment.   (3) Cells replaced by minerals.   (4) Petrified tree.

(1) Bone in sediment.   (2) Water removing minerals.   (3) Leached bone.

Figure 1.7b The drawing above shows how the chemical parts of a bone might be leached away, leaving the fossil in its original shape but very light.

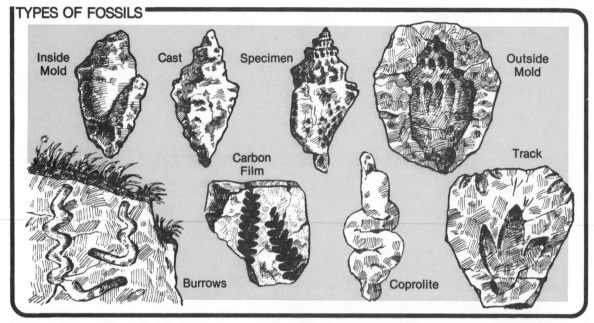

TYPES OF FOSSILS

Inside Mold

Cast

Specimen

Outside Mold

Carbon Film

Track

Burrows

Coprolite

Figure 1.8 Above are the common ways plants and animals are preserved as fossils.

Figure 1.9 (Below) Salamander tracks made in the laboratory under water (a). Fossil vertebrate tracks from the Grand Canyon Coconino sandstone (b). (Courtesy of Dr. Leonard Brand, Loma Linda University)

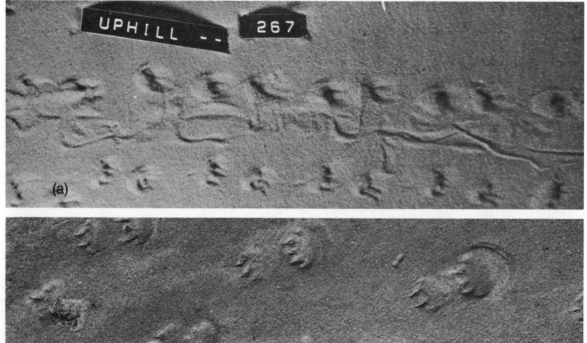

UPHILL -- 267

(a)

(b)

Types of Fossils

Petrified and *leached* **specimens** all contain material from once-living forms. Sometimes, however, an organism disappears entirely, leaving only an impression in the rock called a **mold**. The mold forms an outline of what the living form once looked like. This can be either an inside *mold* or an outside *mold*. Snails and clams are often *preserved* as *molds* (Figure 1.8). If an outside *mold* fills in with another mineral, the filling forms a type of fossil called a **cast.** Sometimes flattened objects like fish or leaves decay, leaving only a **carbon film** as a fossil. These different types of fossils are shown in Figure 1.8.

Tracks or footprints and worm burrows are also called fossils, because they tell us something about once-living creatures. Even dung can be *preserved.* Examining sections of fossilized dung **(coprolites)** under a microscope can help scientists decide what an animal once ate. Just looking at the size of the *coprolite* can help decide how big the animal was! See Figure 1.8.

specimens: objects to be studied

mold: the outline in rock of something once alive (Figure 1.8)

cast: an imprint or copy of a fossil formed of material that fills a mold (Figure 1.8)

carbon film: a thin sheet of carbon that is sometimes left as a fossil trace of a leaf, fish, or other, usually flat, living thing (Figure 1.8)

coprolites: fossilized animal droppings or dung

STOP — REVIEW THE DATA

1. **What is a fossil?**
2. **How are most fossils formed?**
3. **Describe five different types of fossils.**
4. **Explain what an extinct plant or animal is.**
5. **Which of these is most likely to become a fossil: a buffalo shot by a cowboy on the Great Plains; a salmon that dies after laying eggs in its home stream; or a clam buried by a mudslide?**

Geologic Systems

Living things today tend to be found in certain groups or **ecological zones**. Lions and zebras, for instance, are found together on the African grasslands. Cactus and kangaroo rats are found in North American deserts. Clams, snails, and octopi are found along rocky shores.

ecological zone: *(eek-o-'loj-y-kal)* an environment where certain kinds of living things exist, such as a grassland, desert, or pond (Figure 1.10)

Figure 1.10 *An indication of some of the ecological zones on earth today.*

geologic systems: rock units named for the fossils they contain. Names of twelve systems defined in the 1800's are now used worldwide (p. 2 and Figure 1.11)

In a similar way, fossils are also found with each other in groups called **geologic systems**. If a rock layer contains mostly fossils of sea animals called *trilobites* and *lampshells*, then these layers would be a part of the Cambrian ('Kame-bree-an) system.

There are twelve major systems, each identified by the different kinds and numbers of fossils it contains. A system which includes fossils of many dinosaurs and flowering plants is called "Cretaceous" (Kree-'tay-shus). A system rich in remains of coal forest plants is called "Pennsylvanian." However, notice that the Mississippian and Pennsylvanian are sometimes grouped together and called the "Carboniferous" (Kar-bo-'nif-ur-us). Figure 1.11 shows a few of the kinds of life found as fossils in each of the twelve major systems.

(1) CAMBRIAN **(2)** ORDOVICIAN **(3)** SILURIAN **(4)** DEVONIAN **(5)** MISSISSIPPIAN **(6)** PENNSYLVANIAN
(7) PERMIAN **(8)** TRIASSIC **(9)** JURASSIC **(10)** CRETACEOUS **(11)** TERTIARY **(12)** QUATERNARY

Figure 1.11 *Fossils are found in geologic systems (such as the Cambrian), somewhat as living things are found in ecological zones (such as the ponds and woodlands of the hardwood forest zone).*

11

INDEX FOSSILS

CENOZOIC	Quaternary	PECTEN, CALYPTRAPHORUS, VENERICARDIA, NEPTUNEA
	Tertiary	
MESOZOIC	Cretaceous	SCAPHITES, INOCERAMUS
	Jurassic	PERISPHINCTES, NERINEA
	Triassic	TROPHITES, MONOTIS
PALEOZOIC	Permian	LEPTODUS, PARAFUSULINA
	Pennsylvanian	DICTYOCLOSTUS, LOPHOPHYLLIDIUM
	Mississippian	CACTOCRINUS, PROLECANITES
	Devonian	MUCROSPIRIFER, PALMATOLEPUS
	Silurian	CRYSTIPHYLLUM, HEXAMOCERAS
	Ordovician	BATHYURUS, TETRAGRAPTUS
	Cambrian	PARADOXIDES, BILLINGSELLA
PRECAMBRIAN		

Figure 1.12 *Some of the index fossils used for identification of strata. Index fossils must be fairly abundant and restricted to a certain system.*

index fossils: fossils used to identify geologic systems, such as certain trilobites that are markers of Cambrian rocks (Figure 1.10)

Some living things, like clams and snails, are found as fossils in all systems. Dinosaurs are usually found in only three systems. These systems are lumped together as the Mesozoic (Mez-u-'zo-ik) or reptile group. *Trilobites* are usually found in seven systems. These are often lumped together as the Paleozoic (Pa-le-u-'zo-ik) or *trilobite* group.

To identify a system, you either have to consider the numbers of different kinds of fossils or find an **index fossil**. An index fossil is an index, or marker, for a certain system, and is often found in that system and hardly ever in any other. Certain kinds of *trilobites,* for example, are *index fossils* for Cambrian rocks. Finding a *Cactocrinus* (Figure 1.12) means that you are hunting in Mississippian rocks.

Examples of *index fossils* are shown in Figure 1.12. Living index plants and animals are useful today, too. When you find a red-backed salamander, for example, you know you have moved from the oak-hickory to the beech-maple life zone. You do not have to take time to compare percentages of oaks and maple trees.

Sometimes fossils from different *geological systems* and/or different *ecological zones* are mixed together. In the Cumberland Bone Cave in Maryland (Figure 1.13), for example, there are bones of animals that would live today in many different **climatic zones**. Somehow all were washed together, drowned, and buried in a common graveyard. But most of the time, fossils are found only in certain systems. This means that you are not likely to find *trilobites* in the same rock unit with dinosaurs.

climatic zones: zones, such as tropical or temperate, that have the same general weather pattern

Figure 1.13 Here in the Cumberland Bone Cave in Maryland, conditions for fossil formation were ideal. Scientists found many different kinds of fossils that include the remains of animals from different climate zones.

The Geologic Column

Often, but not always, *geologic systems* are found in a certain **vertical** order. Sometimes *trilobites,* coal, and dinosaurs are found in three different rock layers in the same area. When this happens, the *trilobites* will usually be on the bottom, the coal in the middle, and dinosaurs on top. The **geologic column** shows an **ideal** *vertical* order of *geologic systems* (Figures 1.12 and 1.14).

vertical: straight up and down, as opposed to horizontal or across

geologic column: an ideal series of geologic systems meant to show *either* stages in evolution *or* ecological zones of sedimentation

ideal: what a perfect example would show; or, what would occur if an idea were true

gaps: separations that are large and show no real connecting points. There are gaps between fossil kinds and gaps in the geologic column

reversals: rock layers that are "upside down" compared to the ideal geologic column

sequence: expected order or series

trend: things that often happen, but not always

strata: distinctive rock layers, often lying on top of one another

sedimentary zone: layers of fossils with physical features that made them settle out together

Grand Canyon

You cannot go out and see the *geologic column* because it does not exist anywhere. All real rock layers include **gaps** and even **reversals** from this perfect **sequence**. The mile-deep walls of Grand Canyon, for example, include only part of the Cambrian to Permian (Paleozoic) *sequence*. The Ordovician (Or-du-'vish-un) and Silurian (Si-'loor-e-un) systems are missing from this group. If the entire *geologic column* were found in one place, it would be as much as 210 kilometers (130 miles) deep. Actually *sedimentary* rocks in any one place are never more than about 19 – 24 kilometers deep (12 – 15 miles).

The *geologic column* is not a column of rock; it is an idea. But it is an important idea, because it does show a **trend** for rock layers or **strata** to be found in a *vertical sequence.*

What does this *ideal sequence* called the *"geologic column"* mean? Some scientists (evolutionists) say that the systems in the *geologic column* show stages in the evolution of life. They say that this is spread out over millions of years of time. Other scientists (creationists) say that the *geologic systems* represent *ecological* and **sedimentary zones**. It shows how creatures were buried at nearly the same time during a great flood. Chapter 2 will compare these views in more detail.

Figure 1.14 The geologic column is not real in the sense that you can go out and find it somewhere. It does help to understand some things about the usual sequence of various rock layers.

Figure 1.15 The break in the earth's crust at Grand Canyon exposes more of the earth's strata than any other place in the world, but less than half the geologic systems are included; there are gaps in the ideal column sequence.

⑦ PERMIAN	KAIBAB LIMESTONE
	TOROWEAF FORMATION
	COCONINO SANDSTONE
	HERMIT SHALE
⑥ PENNSYLVANIAN	SUPAI GROUP
⑤ MISSISSIPPIAN	REDWALL LIMESTONE
④ DEVONIAN	TEMPLE BUTTE LIMESTONE
① CAMBRIAN	MUAV LIMESTONE
	BRIGHT ANGEL SHALE
	TAPEATS SANDSTONE
PRECAMBRIAN	

REVIEW THE DATA

1. What is an *ecological zone*?
2. What is a *geologic system*?
3. What *geologic system* is noted for its *trilobites*? dinosaurs? coal-forming (carboniferous) plants?
4. Place the systems in Question No. 3 above in the order in which they should be found in the *geologic column*.
5. State the creationist and the evolutionist views of what the *geologic column* means.

warm-blooded: animals, such as birds and dogs, that have a constant body temperature range, independent of their environment

cold-blooded: animals, such as fish and most reptiles, whose body temperature varies with the temperature of their environment

ecological: refers to the kind of environment in which plants and animals live

mammals: animals with hair or fur whose young are nursed on milk, such as cats and dogs

What Do Fossils Mean?

As you have seen, fossils can tell us a lot about life in the past. However, they do not tell us everything. We cannot tell from their bones, for example, whether dinosaurs were **warm-blooded** or **cold-blooded**. We can compare their bone structure to related animals, and we can also compare their **ecological** associations with those of animals living today. Then we can try to guess their past, but we really can never be sure that our guess is right. Since dinosaurs are extinct, we cannot test our ideas. For this reason, scientists are divided on the issue. Some think dinosaurs were probably *warm-blooded* like birds and **mammals**. Most, however, still think they were *cold-blooded* like reptiles living today.

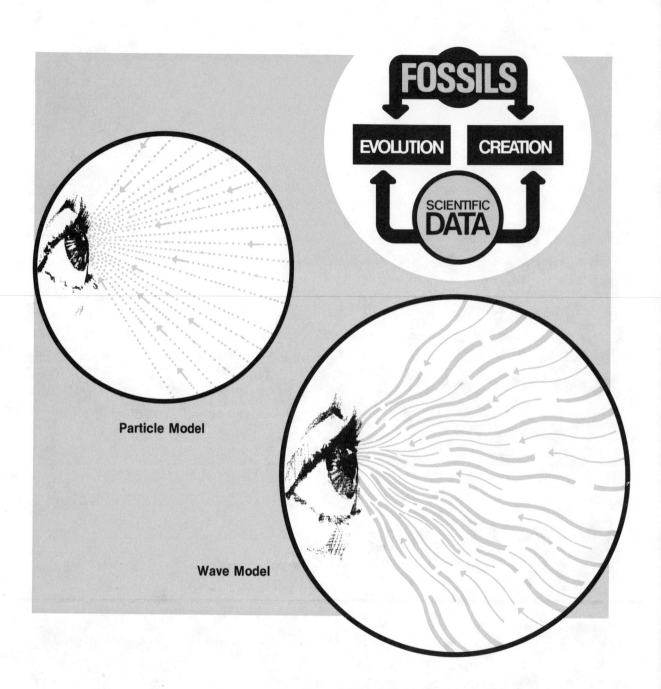

Particle Model

Wave Model

Figure 1.17 *Models are a great help to scientists. They are usually constructed from the best guess that a scientist can make at the time, but he is always ready to change his model when new information comes in.*

Studying fossils, then, is like trying to solve a mystery with only part of the evidence. We have no reports written by human eyewitnesses. We are not able to use the kinds of tests that help us answer many other questions in science.

In such a situation, scientists usually develop **models**. *Models* are broad ideas designed to help them organize and understand the **circumstantial** evidence. At present, for example, no one knows exactly what light is. According to one *model*, light consists of particles; according to another, light is a wave. Thinking in terms of these two *models* helps scientists explain how light acts. These *models* also help construct experiments for finding out more clearly what light really is.

model: an idea or framework used to put data together in a meaningful way

circumstantial: indirect evidence that can be interpreted in more than one way

Two Models for Understanding Fossils

When it comes to interpreting the fossil evidence, we also encounter two scientific *models*: the evolution-**gradualism** *model*, and the creation-**catastrophe** *model*. Scientists holding these two views differ, both on (1) the kinds of life they expect to find as fossils, and on (2) the meaning of the *sequence* of fossils shown in the *geologic column* idea.

gradualism: the idea that fossils and the geologic column have been formed gradually over vast ages of time

catastrophism: the idea that fossils and the geologic column were formed rapidly during a worldwide disaster

According to the Creation–Catastrophe Model:

(1) All the kinds of life we find as fossils can be grouped into separate and distinct created **kinds**. Some kinds have become *extinct,* but most fossils can be classified into the same groups of plants and animals we have today.

kind: a group of animals or plants created separately from all other groups. Variations within a kind are always limited in their extent

(2) The *geologic systems* are broad *ecologic* and *sedimentary zones.* They include fossils of creatures that lived in different places at the same time. The *geologic column* shows the usual *sequence* in which rising flood waters buried plants and animals from these different zones. The creation model would predict what we see in the sediments today.

According to the Evolutionary–Gradualism Model:

(1) Fossils show evolution from simple beginnings to complex forms. They should allow us to trace out the **in-between links** through which one kind of life evolved into another. This record should be a means of seeing evolution from the past.

in-between links: forms of life which are supposed to show how one type of trait changed into another (e.g., scales into feathers) as one kind of life evolved into another (e.g., reptiles into birds)

(2) The *geologic systems* represent creatures living in different time periods, and the geologic column represents stages in the evolution of life over millions of years.

Which model fits the data best—the *creation-catastrophe* model or *gradual evolution?* * The purpose of this book is not to tell you what to think, but to give you a chance to *make up your own mind.*

Let us examine the evidence *objectively.* There were no eyewitnesses, and we cannot run tests on what happened in the past. Our evidence—the fossils—is only *circumstantial.* You should try to decide

* This module deals with fossils, the remains of once-living things. Additional evidence for *creation-catastrophe* and *gradual evolution* is compared in another module in this "Two-Model Series," *Origins: Two Models, Evolution/Creation.*

Figure 1.18 *Creation-catastrophe model.*

Figure 1.19 *Evolution-gradualism model.*

in your own mind whether either case is supported beyond a reasonable doubt.

So let us dig into the fossil evidence. The next chapters go over the facts you need to solve the puzzle. Which model fits the facts best—creation or evolution? Is there enough evidence to decide? Study, think, discuss, and use other resources. See what verdict *you* reach.

Figure 2.1 *Creationists expect to find fossils that are similar to living forms. Some would be extinct, but all would be separate kinds possessing some variations.*

CHAPTER TWO

Kinds of Fossil Life Forms— Evolution or Creation?

Introduction

The study of fossils, called "paleontology" (pay-lee-on-'tol-oh-jee), was just getting started in the 1800's. During that time, Darwin's idea of evolution was replacing creation as the major view among scientists. Many thought that the fossil data would help decide which view was better, evolution or special creation. Certainly the two views produced greatly different ideas about the kinds of life that would be found as fossils.

Let us now try to supply answers to two key questions: **What would we expect to find in the fossil data if creation were true? What would we expect to find in the fossil data if evolution were true?**

Predictions Based on the Creation Model

Creationists believe that all of the basically different kinds of plants and animals were created **mature** by a *supernatural* Creator. Except for extinction, then, each basic kind would appear in the fossil record complete, with no ancestors in an incomplete form. The fossil record should indicate that living things arose suddenly in many different complex forms. According to this idea, we would expect to find fossils of various basic types or groups similar to those we have today. We would expect to find fossils of fishes and fossils of **amphibians**, but we would not expect to find fossils showing fishes gradually changing into *amphibians*. Among the fishes themselves we would expect to find fossils of sharks, eels, swordfish and catfish, with no evidence to suggest that these various kinds were ever anything else.

Among the **invertebrate** fossils we would expect to find worms, jellyfish, sponges, snails, starfish, corals, and lampshells. No fossils of in-between kinds would appear, and we would not expect to find fossils showing that some *invertebrates* gradually changed into fish. In fact, each basically different kind of plant and animal should appear in the fossil record without in-between types.

Figure 2.2 *Are you ready to compare the two models?*

mature: full grown, or able to reproduce

amphibians: animals, such as frogs, that usually live first in water as tadpoles and then on land as adults

invertebrates: animals that do not have a hard backbone, such as worms and starfish

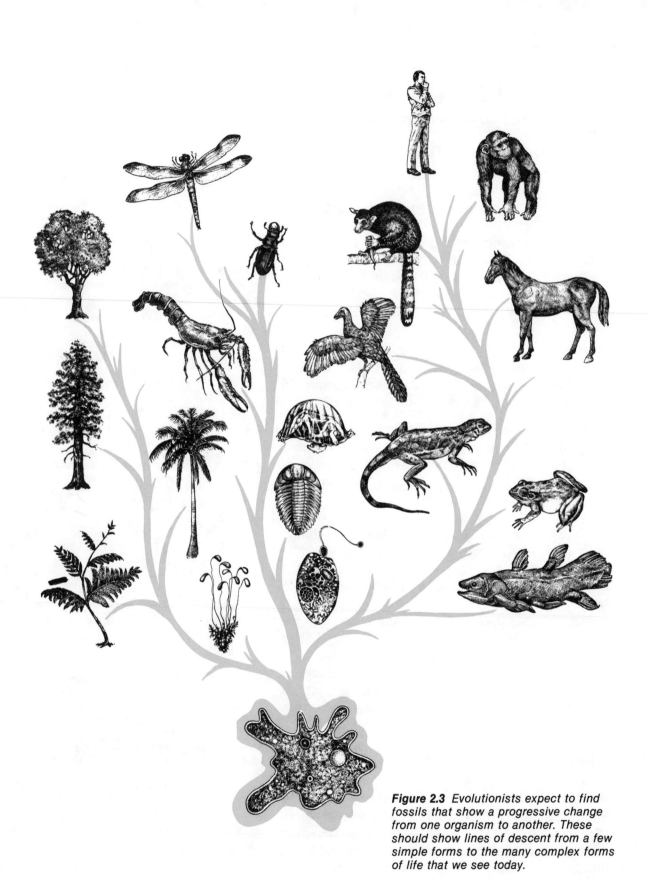

Figure 2.3 *Evolutionists expect to find fossils that show a progressive change from one organism to another. These should show lines of descent from a few simple forms to the many complex forms of life that we see today.*

Predictions Based on the Evolution Model

Evolutionists believe that all living forms have gradually evolved or arisen from one or a few single-celled beginnings. They say that this has happened over many millions of years. Thus, rocks lowest in the column should contain only fossils of very simple forms of life. Fossils further up in the column should show a gradual change from these simple forms of life into more and more complex forms of life. For this reason the fossil record would be expected to produce many in-between or **transitional forms**. Based on the evolution model, one would predict that the fossil record would allow us to trace such things as jellyfish, lampshells, trilobites, nautiloids and other *invertebrates* back to their common ancestor. Scientists should be able to find many types in-between these organisms. We would expect, according to this model, that a close connection of all life from the present to the past could be seen. In fact, we should be able to see a gradual branching tree of life from the very simple to the very complex.

transitional forms: forms of life which are supposed to show how one type of trait changed into another (e.g., scales into feathers) as one kind evolved into another (e.g., reptiles into birds)—same as in-between links

EXAMINING the EVIDENCE

Let us examine the fossil evidence for the major groups of plants and animals. Can you answer the question: "Which model does the data fit best?"

INVERTEBRATES: Animals Without Backbones

The vast majority of animal fossils are shells, molds, casts, and other remains of *invertebrates*. These animals without backbones include those found in Figure 2.4.

(1) Crinoids, **(2)** Jellyfish, **(3)** Sponges, **(4)** Starfish, **(5)** Trilobites, **(6)** Nautiloid, **(7)** Clam, **(8)** Brachiopods, **(9)** Sea urchins, **(10)** Segmented worm, **(11)** Snails, **(12)** Coral.

Figure 2.4 *Invertebrate sea life reconstructed from Ordovician fossils found near Madison, Indiana. Do you recognize forms similar to those living today? . . . extinct forms?*

Near Madison, Indiana, whole hillsides are covered with such fossils. Creek beds seem to be paved with them. Millions of specimens from thousands of tons of rock have been collected from around the world. What does this evidence appear to tell us? Examine the evidence in Figure 2.4.

Figure 2.5 Diorama of Cambrian sea life. How are these plants and animals at the "base" of the geologic column similar to those today? How are they different?

Figure 2.6 Scallop shells and two kinds of snails. One of each pair is a fossil, and the other is a modern shell.

If you have seen the kinds of creatures that live in the oceans today, you might think that Figure 2.5 is a picture of life off the coast of some South Sea island. But it is not. Figure 2.5, a photograph of a display in the American Museum of Natural History, shows what sea life looked like when Cambrian fossils were alive.

The **Cambrian** is at the bottom of the *geologic column* (Figure 2.7). According to the evolution model, *Cambrian* life forms show the first forms of life on earth to leave many fossil remains.

What do we really find in *Cambrian* rock according to known scientific data? Do there appear to be any kinds of fossils that would be intermediate between clams and snails?

Cambrian: the bottom of the geologic column, *either* fossils of the first stage of evolution (evolution model) *or* the life zone buried first in a great catastrophe (creation model)

Figure 2.7 *Many complex invertebrates are found in Cambrian strata; the ones living today are similar, but show less variety. What does this comparison mean to you?*

The largest and most complex of all the *invertebrates,* members of the **octopus group,** have eyes much like ours. They are also found right from the beginning of the *sequence* in *Cambrian* rock. These *Cambrian* forms **(nautiloids)** have a long, straight shell (reaching 9 feet in length!), while the modern pearly *Nautilus* has a coiled shell.

Some fossil corals have **shelves** and modern ones do not. Fossil snails have minor differences in their twists and spines that allow them to be **classified** as different species of snails. All these creatures are easily seen as snails, and appear much like the modern forms we see.

Fossils also show that a greater variety of sea life existed in the past than we have today. All of the trilobites and most of the *lampshells* **(brachiopods)** have become extinct. Although a few sea lilies **(crinoids)** survive in the deep ocean, many that once formed vast undersea gardens are gone forever. Of all the large and complex squid-like animals, only the pearly *Nautilus* and a few species of shell-less squids and octopi remain.

If we compare fossil sea creatures with forms living today we would probably ask, "What happened?" "Where did all the nautiloids go?. . .the sea lilies?. . .the trilobites?. . .the lampshells?" Among the *invertebrates,* only the clam and snail group is present in greater variety today than as fossils.

Paleontologists have searched Precambrian rocks intensely for ancestors of the Cambrian animals. Daniel Axelrod, American paleontologist, has stated that this is an unsolved problem. After discussing the varied types found in the Cambrian, Axelrod went on to say that their ancestors are nowhere to be found. He mentions that there are many rocks in existence which should contain these fossil ancestors, if they existed.

More recently, fossils of groups of soft-bodied invertebrates have been found in various places around the world. It is generally believed, by evolutionists, that these creatures lived before the animals found in Cambrian rocks. These creatures have been termed the Ediacaran Fauna. It was at first believed that these creatures may have been

octopus group: the octopus, squid, and other sea animals with muscular bodies, long tentacles, eyes, and sometimes a shell

nautiloid: a squid-like animal with a straight or coiled shell similar to the living pearly *Nautilus* (p. 28)

shelves: floors formed across the coral chamber as the chamber grows taller

classified: placed into groups that are ordered in some way

brachiopod: *('brak-e-o-pod)* an animal with arms of tentacles living inside a top and bottom shell; a lampshell (Figure 1.4)

crinoids: sea lilies; members of the starfish group whose "stems" are often found as fossils (Figure 2.4)

"One of the major unsolved problems of geology and evolution is the occurrence of diversified, multicellular marine invertebrates in Lower Cambrian rocks on all the continents and their absence in rocks of greater age."[1]

"However, when we turn to examine the Precambrian rocks for the forerunners of these early Cambrian fossils, they are nowhere to be found. Many thick (over 5,000 feet) sections of sedimentary rock are now known to lie in unbroken succession below strata containing the earliest Cambrian fossils. These sediments apparently were suitable for the preservation of fossils because they are often identical with overlying rocks which are fossiliferous, yet no fossils are found in them."[1]

ancestral to the Cambrian animals. Subsequent research has shown that they are so different from the Cambrian animals, they could not possibly be their ancestors. Evolutionists still admit that no ancestors have been found for a single one of the very complex invertebrates found in Cambrian rocks. Each appears fully formed at their first appearance. Some evolutionists have termed this the "major mystery of the history of life."

Other evolutionists have claimed that ancestors to the Cambrian animals did not leave fossils, because they were all soft-bodied. Creation scientists point out, however, that fossils of many soft-bodied animals have been found, including fossils of microscopic, single-celled, soft-bodied bacteria and algae. Surely, they insist, if fossils of bacteria can be found, fossils of everything between the single-celled first forms of life and the complex invertebrates could be found. It would also be astounding if all of the Cambrian animals with hard parts suddenly evolved hard parts approximately at the same time. Creation scientists ask what greater evidence for creation could the rocks give than this sudden outburst of a great variety of complex invertebrates for which no ancestors have been found? Which model of origins does this evidence seem to support?

INTERPRET THE DATA

Figure 2.8 What do invertebrate fossils tell us about the history of life?

1. **Creationists believe that many different living organisms have existed, since creation, as distinct kinds. Does our knowledge of *Cambrian* fossils offer any support for this view?**

2. **Evolution is usually pictured as a progressive development from simple to more complex and different forms of life. Are *Cambrian trilobites* simple animals? What about *Cambrian nautiloids*? Do *Cambrian snails* and *clams* seem simpler than modern snails and clams?**

3. **We find many more different kinds of *invertebrate* sea animals as fossils than those which are living today. Does this pattern of extinction tend to favor evolution, or creation? Explain.**

4. **Axelrod reports that invertebrate animals appear suddenly in *Cambrian* rocks. How do creationists interpret this? . . . evolutionists?**

5. **Compare the invertebrate fossil data with the predictions based on the evolution and creation models. Which model seems to fit most facts the best? Give examples of the strongest evidence to support your view.**

PLANTS

Did you ever wonder what kinds of plants lived on the earth when dinosaurs did? When it comes to flowering plants, you might be surprised to hear such familiar names as oak, maple, willow, sassafrass, magnolia, fig and palm. Fossil flowering plants are very much like those we have today, and they are found in great numbers in Cretaceous rock. There are no clues as to how they might have originated from other kinds of plants. They appear **abruptly** in the fossil record in great variety without *transitional forms* linking them to other plants.

abruptly: quickly and without prior notice

Darwin was aware of these facts. He called the origin of flowering plants "an abominable mystery." More than 100 years later Harold C. Bold wrote in his textbook, *Morphology of Plants*, that these words are still true.

Of course, missing links might still be found. But what about all the many fossil plants we have already found? Professor Corner at Cambridge University wrote: ". . . to the **unprejudiced**, the fossil record of plants is in favor of [special] creation."[3]

"In spite of advances in our knowledge of comparative floral morphology, flower structure, and of the fossil record, and in spite of the publication of many pages of speculation on this subject, Darwin's words still eloquently summarize the current state of our knowledge."[2]

unprejudiced: without having some prejudice or bias; when a person's mind is not made up ahead of time

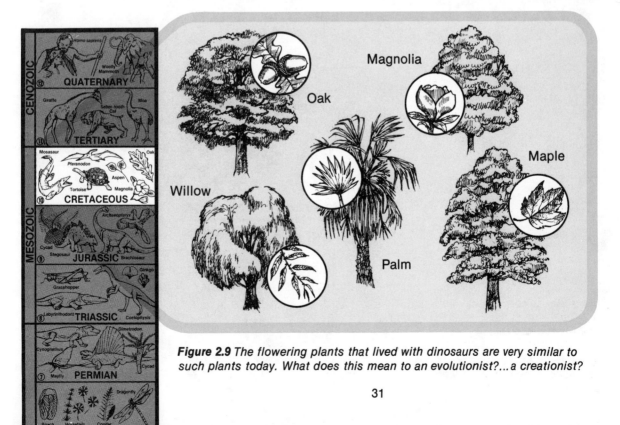

Figure 2.9 The flowering plants that lived with dinosaurs are very similar to such plants today. What does this mean to an evolutionist?...a creationist?

Figure 2.10 shows other plants that are found abundantly as fossils. Most are grouped along with the modern plants, and anyone having seen ferns today would easily know fossil fern leaves, which are common. Varieties within these groups differ in minor ways from those living today. Because of **extinction** there is even a greater variety among fossil plants than among living forms.

extinction: becoming extinct; being found only as a fossil and not found alive today

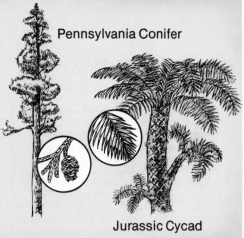

Figure 2.10 Above are two cone-bearing plants common both today and as fossils.

Figure 2.11 Ferns and fern allies commonly found as fossils. Only a few are still living.

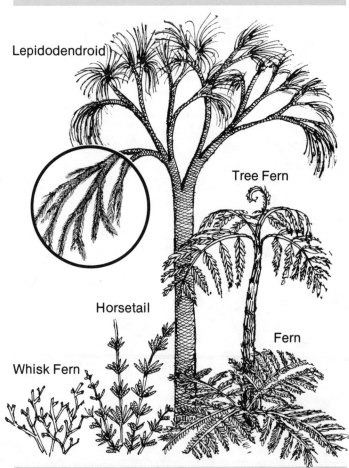

fern allies: plants that look and reproduce somewhat like ferns. Many kinds, now extinct, are found as fossils in coal (Figure 2.11)

horsetails: a common name for fern allies like the living *Equisetum*. Most, including giant forms, are extinct

whisk fern: a living member of a group of fern allies almost all extinct (Figure 2.11)

There is a group of plants called **fern allies** that were very hard hit by *extinction*. These plants, along with ferns and some special seed plants, appear as distinct groups in the fossil record. Many members of these groups reached the size of large trees in the "coal forests," as shown in Figure 2.10. However, only a few different kinds of *fern allies* are still alive today. These include "living fossils," such as **horsetails** and **whisk ferns** shown in Figure 2.11.

No one is sure why such well-**adapted** plants became *extinct.* Many creationists believe the atmosphere of the pre-Flood world contained much more water vapor and higher levels of carbon dioxide. This would give the whole earth a warm climate from pole to pole. Some, however, do not accept a vapor canopy idea. They do agree, nevertheless, that fossils from almost all systems shared a much milder worldwide climate (Figure 2.12). Perhaps because of the climate change, a large portion of the more tropical plants (including many ferns and *fern allies)* died out, but those better *adapted* to seasonal cold could survive this change.

It seems that only the percents of different plant types have changed. There were once many more ferns and *fern allies* compared to seed plants. Fossil plants are classified into distinct types, and these do not show past links. In fact, except for extinction, fossil plants are identified from the very

Figure 2.12 *The evidence seems to indicate a worldwide mild climate at one time. The reasons for this are not agreed upon, although some creationists suggest a vapor canopy may have played a role.*

adapted: suited to its environment

algae: non-woody green plants that usually live in water

beginning with the same groups we use for plants living today.

This is also true for water plants called **"algae."** Harold Bold writes, "fossilized algae are in almost every case largely similar to . . . present-day algae." He adds that all the major groups of algae are found in lowest *Cambrian* rock.[2]

STOP

INTERPRET THE DATA

1. How do you think evolutionists would interpret our knowledge of fossil plants? . . . creationists?

2. Do you suppose that future research may yet uncover evolutionary links between plant groups?

3. Many plants that form our vast coal deposits have become *extinct*.
   a. How would you explain this?
   b. How might a creationist explain this extinction?
   c. How would an evolutionist explain extinction?

marine: refers to salt water environment

vertebrates: animals with hard backbones, such as birds and mammals

VERTEBRATES: Animals With Backbones

Marine invertebrates and *algae* are found lower in the *geologic column*, and the **vertebrates** and land plants are found farther up in the column (see

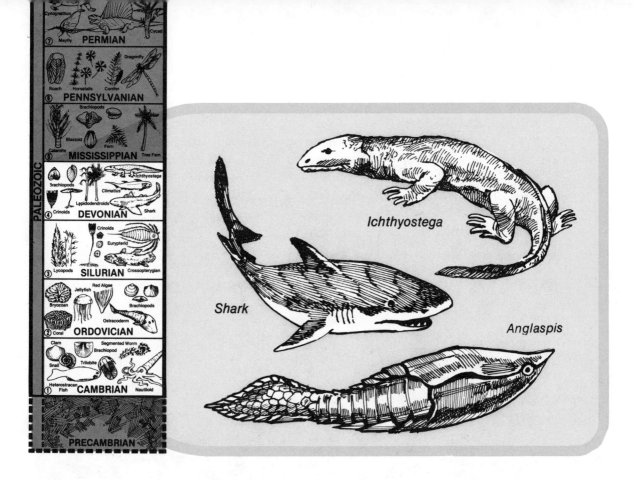

Figure 2.13 In the geologic column (left), there is a sequence from invertebrates to fish to land animals. According to evolution, some fish changed into amphibians (right). What does this series mean to a creationist?

Figure 2.14 An "evolutionary tree," showing a concept of relationship among vertebrate groups.

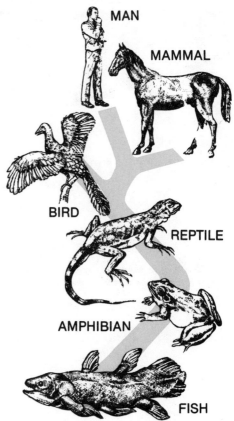

Figure 2.13). Does this represent an evolutionary or an ecological series?

No fossils of invertebrates or plants are widely held to be evolutionary in-between forms from one major group to another, but, when it comes to the *vertebrates*, we see some fossils that *are* thought to be in-between forms, or connecting links between one group and another. According to evolutionists, these fossils show that some fish evolved into *amphibians,* some *amphibians* into *reptiles,* some *reptiles* into birds, and other *reptiles* into *mammals.* (including man). This is shown in Figure 2.14.

35

Origin of Fish

A few fossils are offered to show how one *vertebrate* group may have evolved into another, but no fossils have ever been found to show how the first *vertebrates,* the fishes, may have evolved from *invertebrate* ancestors.

Vertebrate Paleontology is a book written by the respected paleontologist, A. S. Romer. He writes that the origin of bony fishes is a "dramatically sudden one." He claims that a "common ancestor of the bony fish groups is unknown." He also states that **placoderms**, an extinct group of fishes, pose a deep problem for evolution. He even suggests that evolution would be better off without them.

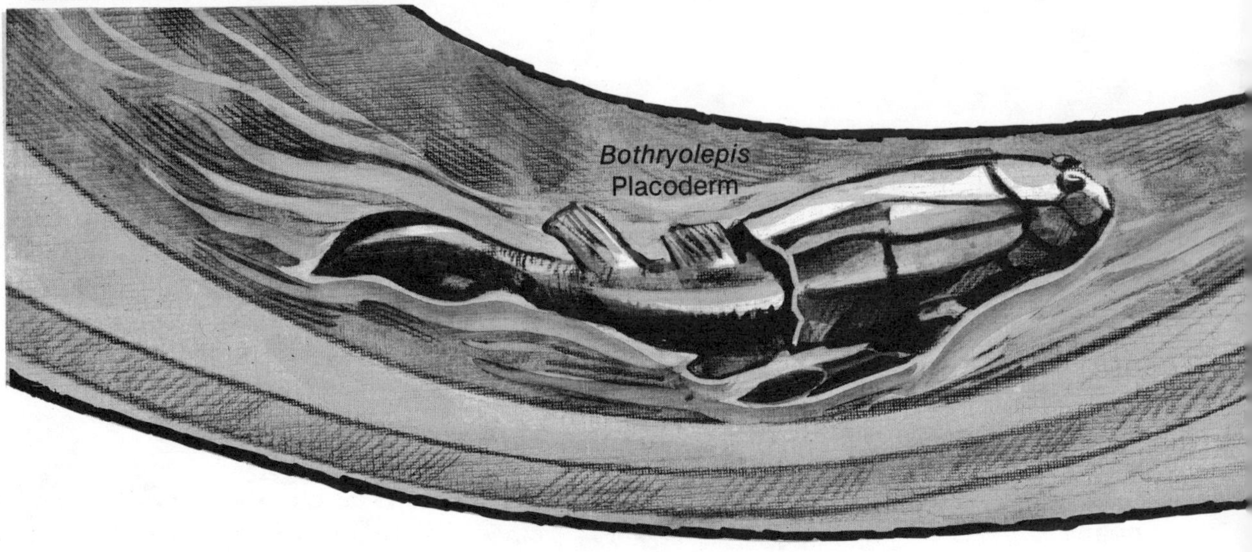

> "We would expect 'generalized' forms that would fit neatly into our preconceived evolutionary picture. Do we get them in the placoderms? Not at all. Instead, we find a series of wildly impossible types which do not fit into any proper pattern; which do not, at first sight, seem to come from any possible source or to be appropriate ancestors to any later or more advanced types. In fact, one tends to feel that these placoderms, making up such an important part of the Devonian fish story, is an incongruous episode; it would have simplified the situation [for evolution] if they had never existed!"[4]

Bothryolepis
Placoderm

placoderms: extinct fish with bony plates

Figure 2.15 *The placoderm, shown above, is a puzzling extinct fish.*

> "But whatever ideas authorities may have on the subject, the lung-fishes, like every other major group of fishes that I know, have their origins firmly based in *nothing*..."[5]

In addition to this, Errol White, an expert on fishes, says that the origins of fish groups are based upon nothing.

Fish are fairly common in Devonian rock and were at one time thought to be absent from Cambrian rock. Many evolutionary scientists suggest that fish evolved from the *invertebrates* during Cambrian times. At the present time, however, there is no evidence of this in the fossil record. F. D. Ommany, another student of the fishes, supports the view that there is no evidence for these changes.

Since fossils of fish have now been found in upper Cambrian rock, the search for their ancestors must be pushed back into lower Cambrian or Precambrian rocks. But **Precambrian** rocks, almost entirely lacking in fossils, seem to offer little hope for success.

Precambrian: rocks, many are sedimentary but usually without fossils, generally found below Cambrian rocks

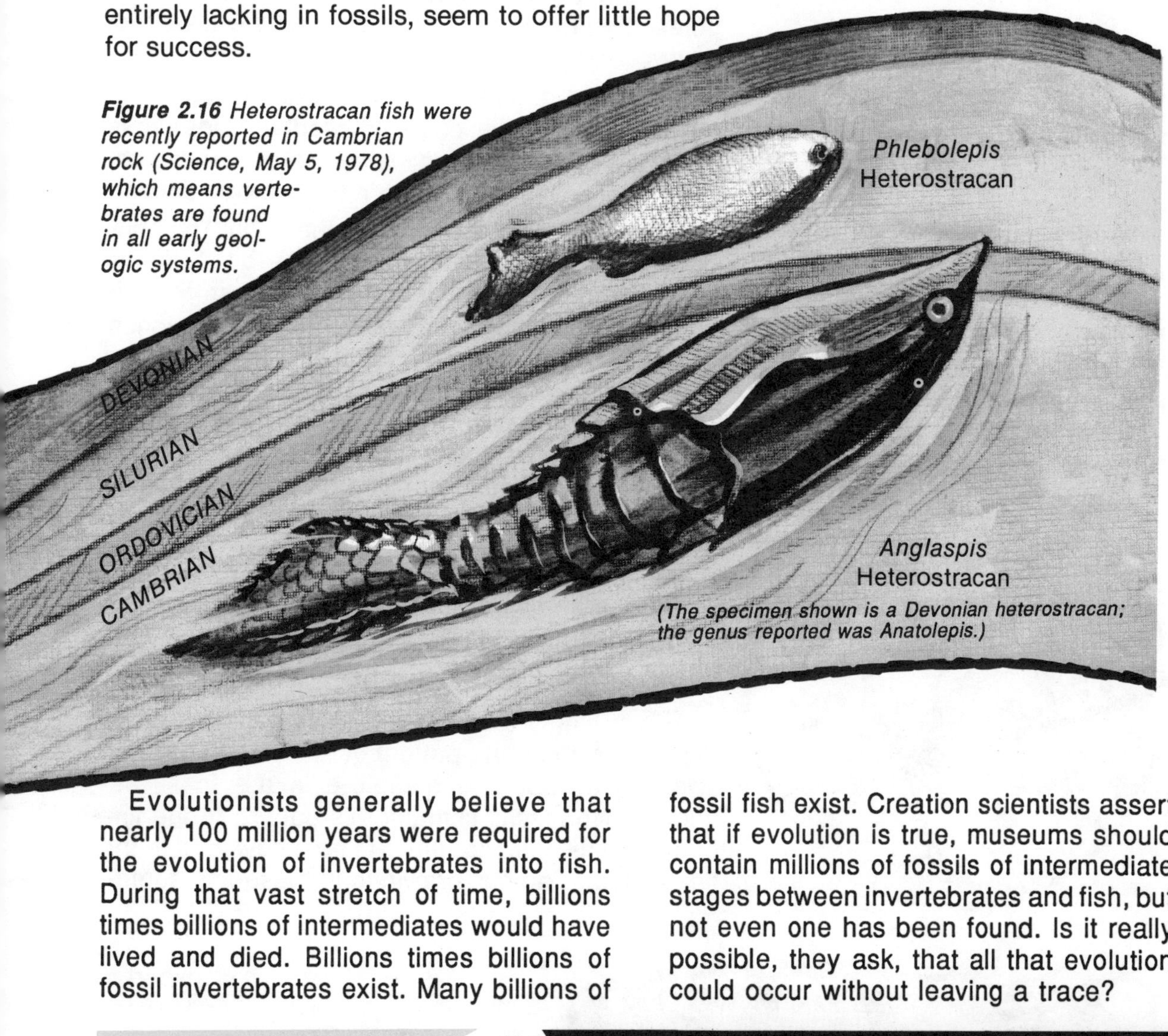

Figure 2.16 *Heterostracan fish were recently reported in Cambrian rock (Science, May 5, 1978), which means vertebrates are found in all early geologic systems.*

DEVONIAN

SILURIAN

ORDOVICIAN

CAMBRIAN

Phlebolepis
Heterostracan

Anglaspis
Heterostracan

(The specimen shown is a Devonian heterostracan; the genus reported was Anatolepis.)

Evolutionists generally believe that nearly 100 million years were required for the evolution of invertebrates into fish. During that vast stretch of time, billions times billions of intermediates would have lived and died. Billions times billions of fossil invertebrates exist. Many billions of fossil fish exist. Creation scientists assert that if evolution is true, museums should contain millions of fossils of intermediate stages between invertebrates and fish, but not even one has been found. Is it really possible, they ask, that all that evolution could occur without leaving a trace?

STOP

INTERPRET THE DATA

1. What would creationist? . . . evolutionists infer from our knowledge of fossil fishes?
2. Recent research turned up fossil fish in Cambrian rock. What predictions for further research do you think creationists would make? . . . evolutionists?

Origin of Amphibia: Land-Water Animals

Living amphibians, such as frogs and salamanders, are usually slimy-skinned animals that lead "double lives." First, they are swimming, gill-breathing tadpoles, then they live as four-legged, lung-breathing adults.

Amphibian origins center on two groups of fossils: (1) Lobe-finned fishes called **crossopterygians** (cross-op-ter'ij-uns), and (2) *Ichthyostega* (Ick-the-o-'stag-uh), the first or lowest amphibian in the geologic column.

Figure 2.17 shows the lobe-finned fish. The bone pattern in its fin is somewhat similar to the pattern in your arm and in the leg of a frog. First, there is one bone attached to the body; next, are two bones, as in your forearm; finally, there is a group of small bones with **radiating** lines of bones to the end, somewhat like your wrist and hand. Lobe-finned fish are still alive today (Figure 2.18), and include forms that can use their swim bladders somewhat like lungs. These fishes also had complex, arch-type vertebrae (backbones) like those found in *Ichthyostega*. Teeth and some parts of the skull are similar, and some are not. On the basis of these likenesses, evolutionists **infer** that amphibians evolved from these fishes.

As you study these fossils, also consider these data: First, the bone pattern in the lobe-finned fish appears abrupt and complete in the fossil sequence. No fossils connect this pattern to the fins of other fish. Second, there is no elbow joint in the fin. Although artists' drawings in museums some-

crossopterygian: *(cross-op-ter-'ij-un)* lobe-finned fish thought closest to amphibians by many evolutionists

Ichthyostega: *(ick-the-o-'stag-uh)* the extinct amphibian thought closest to the fish by many evolutionists

radiating: going out from a single source, like spokes from the center of a wheel

infer: to draw conclusions from incomplete evidence

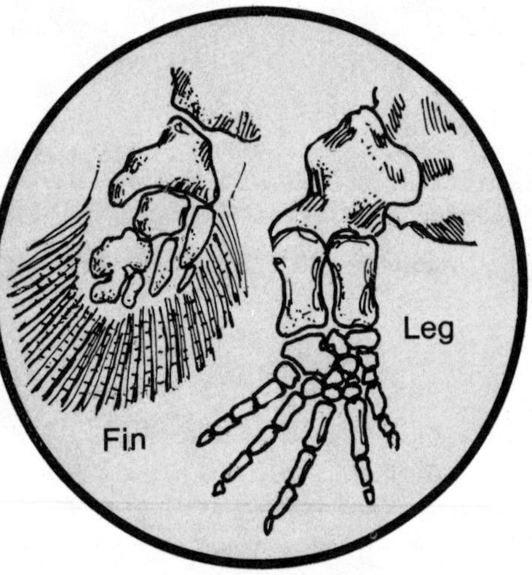

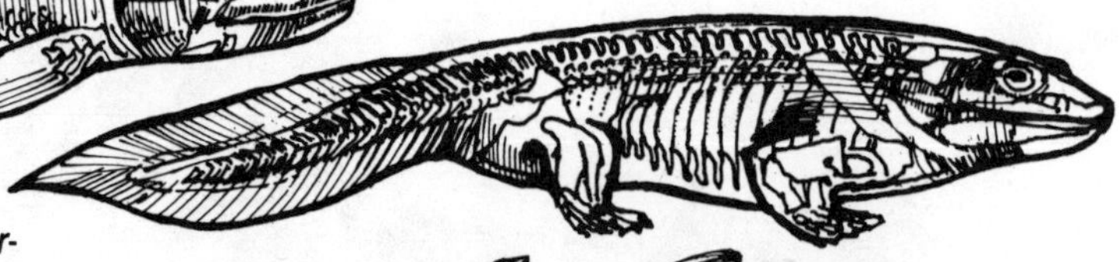

Leg

Fin

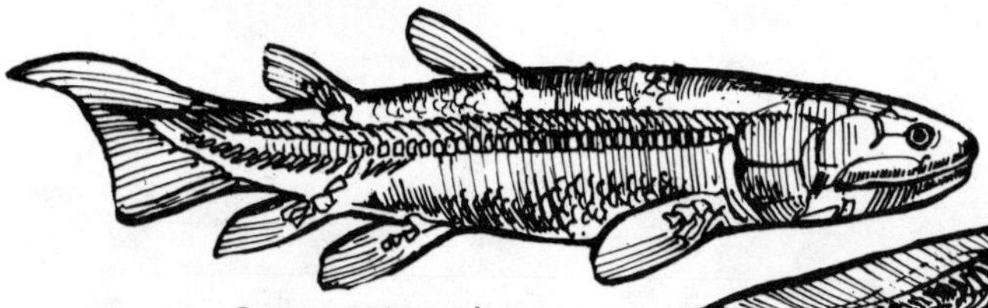

Figure 2.17 *Note similarities and differences in the bone pattern (circled, upper left) for the fin of a crossopterygian fish and the leg of a fossil amphibian, Ichthyostega.*

Figure 2.18 *The coelacanth, a crossopterygian, has been found alive off the coast of Madagascar.*

Crossopterygian

Ichthyostega

Coelacanth

times show this **inferred** in-between form, no fossils of fish with jointed fins have been found. Third, the pelvic (hip) bone of the fish is small. This bone is loosely attached in muscle, and does not connect to the back bone. Fourth, three other orders of amphibians appear in the geologic system immediately following the system containing *Ichthyostega*, and all of these have spool-type vertebrae. Such vertebrae are quite different from those of both *Ichthyostega* and the lobe-finned fish. Finally, the "living fossil" lobe-finned fish (Figure 2.18), is adapted for life in the deep sea, and does not use its fins for "walking." Creationists say, therefore, that lobe-finned fish and *Ichthyostega* are distinct kinds. Instead of descent from a common ancestor, they show creation according to a common plan.

Here is a tough case. The similarities seem to support evolution; the differences seem to support creation. Use the questions below to help you figure out which model seems to fit the data best.

inferred: having drawn conclusions from incomplete evidence

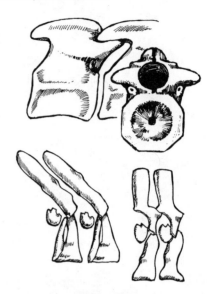

Figure 2.19 *Compare spool type vertebrae (above) with arch type (below).*

INTERPRET THE DATA

Compare the skeleton of the *crossopterygian* fish to that of the *amphibian Ichthyostega* in Figure 2.17.

1. **To what are the pelvic bones of this fish attached? To what are the pelvic bones of this *amphibian* attached? What would have to happen to change one into the other? List your ideas.**

2. **Does the fish seem well suited to life in the water? Does the *amphibian* seem well suited to life on land? Can you imagine how the change from water life to land life took place? Look up ideas in your library. What parts of a lobe-finned fish support evolution? What parts support creation? In your opinion, who has the strongest case? Give your reasons.**

Snake

Lizard

Turtle

Crocodile

Figure 2.20 *Living examples of those scaly-skinned animals, the reptiles.*

Seymouria: *(say-'more-e-uh)* the extinct reptile thought closest to the amphibians by many evolutionists

Origin of Reptiles: Scaly-Skinned Animals

Living reptiles include lizards, snakes, turtles and crocodiles. These are mostly dry, scaly-skinned animals that lay leathery-skinned eggs on land.

Figure 2.21 shows the skeleton of **Seymouria** (Say-'more-e-uh), a fossil reptile with a skeleton similar in some ways to that of amphibians. *Seymouria* is sometimes offered as an evolutionary link between amphibians and reptiles, but it occurs in the geologic column "after" other reptiles. You can see this presents a problem of sorts. Can you think of some answers to this problem that would satisfy an evolutionist? Creationists would say the fossils show that reptiles have always been reptiles.

Actually, we should not expect fossils to help us decide whether amphibians evolved into reptiles. Vertebrate fossils are mostly bones and teeth, and there are few skeletal differences today between certain groups of amphibians and reptiles. However, we can easily see that living amphibians and living

40

CENOZOIC

QUATERNARY
Giraffe · Saber-tooth Cat · Moa · Mammoth

TERTIARY

MESOZOIC

CRETACEOUS
Mosasaur · Pteranodon · Aspen · Tortoise · Turtle · Magnolia · Oak

JURASSIC
Archaeopteryx · Cycad · Stegosaur · Brachiosaur

TRIASSIC
Grasshopper · Ginkgo · Labyrinthodont · Coelophysis

PALEOZOIC

PERMIAN
Cynognathus · Dimetrodon · Mayfly · Cycad

PENNSYLVANIAN
Roach · Horsetails · Conifer · Dragonfly

MISSISSIPPIAN
Brachiopods · Blastoid · Calamite · Fern · Tree Fern

DEVONIAN
Brachiopods · Ichthyostega · Climatius · Crinoids · Lepidodendroids · Shark

SILURIAN
Crinoids · Eurypterid · Lycopods · Crossopterygian

Seymouria
(about 30" long)

Hylonomus
(about 30" long)

Figure 2.21 More "advanced" reptiles (Hylonomus) are found lower in the geologic column than "primitive" forms (Seymouria) that more closely resemble amphibians. What does this mean to an evolutionist? . . . a creationist?

reptiles are different groups. We see that young reptiles look much like adults when they hatch out of eggs laid on land. Amphibians start as tadpoles that live in the water and they must change into land-dwelling adults. The actual differences between these two groups are really great.

If we could see the soft parts and life cycle of *Seymouria*, then, we might be able to tell easily whether it was reptile or amphibian. Fossils just cannot give us that kind of information. However, fossils *do* tell us much about a special group of reptiles, the dinosaurs.

Figure 2.22 Reptile eggs hatch into young that resemble adults; amphibian eggs hatch into tadpoles that must change greatly to become adults.

41

Figure 2.23 *Various kinds of dinosaurs have been found as complete and almost complete skeletons.*

42

Dinosaurs –Those Terrible Lizards

Dinosaur fossils are found on every continent of the world, including the subcontinent of Australia. Their fossils are found as far north as the north shore of Alaska and as far south as Antarctica. They appear in great variety, and in many sizes. Some are as small as chickens and some weigh over 50 tons. Vast fossil graveyards of dinosaurs are found in North America, Africa, Asia, and other places.

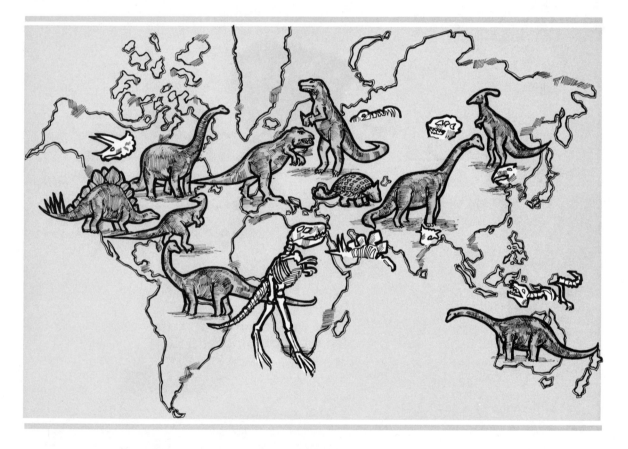

Dinosaurs are found in only three *geologic systems:* Triassic, Jurassic, and Cretaceous, Figure 2.25. Evolutionists lump these three systems into the Mesozoic Era, or "Age of Reptiles." They treat Mesozoic rocks as time periods. Creationists also lump the dinosaur systems into a Mesozoic zone, or zone of reptiles. They treat Mesozoic rocks as ecological and sedimentary zones. Thus, the three Mesozoic systems are either the times or the places that dinosaurs ruled the scene.

Figure 2.24 *Dinosaur fossils have been found all over the world.*

Figure 2.25 *Dinosaurs are index fossils because they are found in the distinct portions of the column (the Mesozoic), as shown.*

Why did dinosaurs become extinct? This question has puzzled scientists for many years. Some blame their extinction on radiation from an exploding star. Others blame it on a change in climate or even a virus "dinosaur plague." A few even suggest that they died of constipation because a laxative plant in their diet became *extinct*! Several scientists, both creationists and evolutionists, believe extinction of dinosaurs was most likely caused by massive flooding of the continents. This, of course, greatly changed the environment—so much, in fact, that they could not survive.

Many kinds of dinosaurs have been found. Figure 2.25 shows: *Triceratops*, which has a well-protected head with horns; *Stegosaurus*, with long spikes on its tail and broad plates on its back; *Trachodon*, a duck-billed dinosaur; *Ankylosaurus*, an armored dinosaur; *Tryannosaurus rex*, a huge meat-eating dinosaur; and *Brachiosaurus*, the largest dinosaur of all, weighing up to 100 tons and standing as high as 50 feet.

Could all these dinosaurs have evolved from a reptile of some kind? Although there are different views among experts, Dr. Barry Cox said that the origin of dinosaurs is almost as much a mystery as their extinction.

Creationists note that in every case each basic type of dinosaur appears abruptly and without in-between forms. For example, a gradual formation cannot be found for the spikes and plates of *Stegosaurus*, for the bony armor and tail club of *Ankylosaurus*, or for the duckbill of *Trachodon*.

> "Although many pages have been written discussing the mystery of the extinction of the dinosaurs, almost as much uncertainty surrounds their origin or origins."[6]

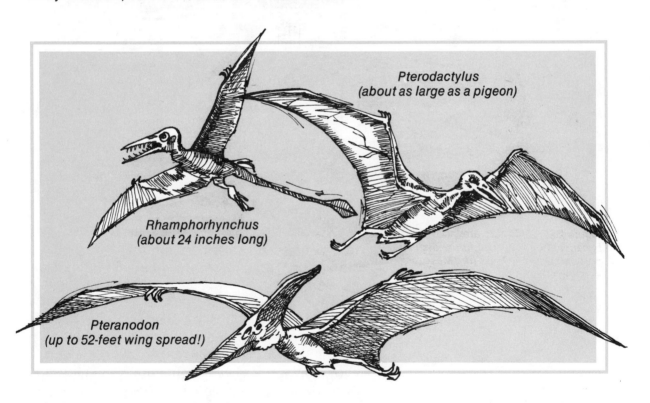

Pterodactylus (about as large as a pigeon)

Rhamphorhynchus (about 24 inches long)

Pteranodon (up to 52-feet wing spread!)

Figure 2.26 *Several distinct kinds of flying reptiles ("pterodactyls") are known as fossils.*

Flying Reptiles – Those Winged Monsters

Strange flying reptiles once lived on the earth. One form was only about one and one-half feet long, but *Pteranodon* had a wingspread of up to 52 feet (the same as an F–4 fighter jet!). All flying reptiles had a long fourth "finger" to support the wing membrane. Unlike other reptiles, *Pteranodon* also had a three-foot long toothless beak and a long, bony crest. While some feel that these flying reptiles might have come from non-flying reptiles (such as thecodonts), many reject the idea. Dr. E. C. Olson, a paleontologist, has stated that there is no trace of a form in between non-flying and flying reptiles.[7] Others feel that this is what would be expected, if flying reptiles were created.

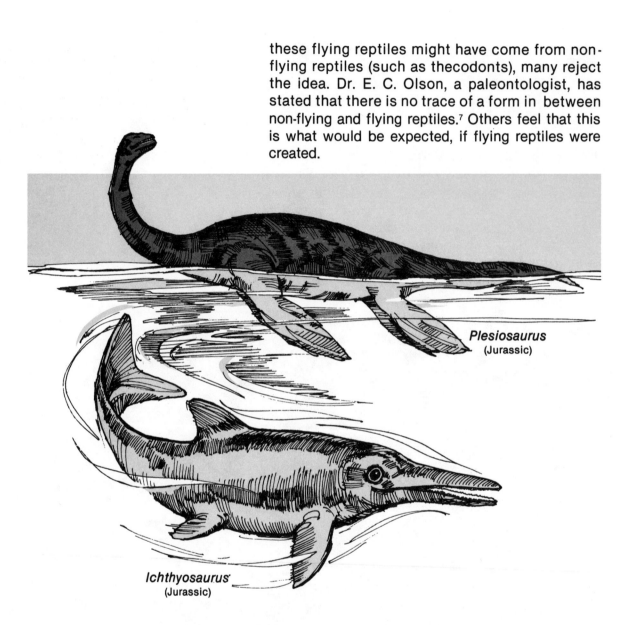

Plesiosaurus
(Jurassic)

Ichthyosaurus
(Jurassic)

Figure 2.27 Many marine reptiles have been found. The plesiosaur (above) and the ichthyosaur (below) are examples. Both are extinct.

Almost as strange as the flying reptiles, but designed for an entirely different habitat, were the marine reptiles. They are now extinct, but their fossilized remains show that they were reptiles, not fish. *Plesiosaurs* had paddles, instead of feet and legs; the *Ichthyosaurs* were quite fishlike, and swam much like most fish do today (Figure 2.27). Evolutionists believe these marine reptiles evolved from land-dwelling forms. Creationists believe they are distinct kinds, descended from created ancestors. No intermediates between land reptiles and marine reptiles have been found.

EXAMINE THE DATA

1. What is the most important difference between living reptiles and living amphibians? Can we expect fossils to tell us about the origin of this difference?

2. Evolutionists believe that some amphibians must have given up their tadpole stage and become able to lay eggs (in shells) on land. Look in other sources. Are there any good theories about how this change could have occurred? Is this a problem for evolution, support for creation, neither, or both?

3. *Seymouria* is found higher in the column than "more advanced" reptiles. What does this mean to evolutionists? . . . creationists?

4. What are some interesting facts about dinosaurs on which creationists and evolutionists agree? What differences are there in the interpretation of some of these facts?

5. Flying reptiles and marine reptiles have skeletons very different from land-dwelling reptiles. Are there fossils to show how land forms might have evolved into flying and swimming forms? How do evolutionists respond to the data we have on hand? . . . creationists?

Origin of Birds – Those Feathered Friends

We cannot expect fossils to tell us much about the origin of reptiles from amphibians, but we should expect any gradual change from reptiles to birds to leave clear in-between forms. There are big differences in the skeletons of reptiles and birds. Feathers and scales (or their impressions) are also found as fossils. At this point we meet the most famous fossil claimed as support for evolution: *Archaeopteryx* (Ark-ee-'op-ter-iks).

Figure 2.28 *The famous Berlin fossil specimen of Archaeopteryx (a), and an artist's conception (b).*

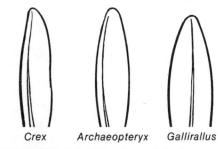

Crex   Archaeopteryx   Gallirallus

Figure 2.29 *Flight feathers of Archaeopteryx (center) resemble those of strong flyers (left) rather than those of non-flyers (right).*

Among the few specimens of *Archaeopteryx* that have been found, there is a very good specimen. The fossil imprint (from the Jurassic Solnhofen limestone in Germany) and an artist's reconstruction are shown in Figures 2.28a and 2.28b.

Notice the bird-like features: feathers, wings and a bill. But notice also the reptile-like features: a long, bony tail; claws on the wings; and teeth in the bill. Lack of a breastbone and backbones that are not fused are also more reptile-like than bird-like.

Thus, *Archaeopteryx* appears to be a perfect example of an evolutionary link. Or is it?

We are sure that by now there are many questions going through your mind. Let us look at some of the problems that arise in understanding *Archaeopteryx*.

According to some, feathers evolved from reptile scales. However, *Archaeopteryx* has fully developed feathers of several different kinds. There are data that show these feathers to be just like flying birds and not like non-flying birds (Figure 2.29). It appears that *Archaeopteryx* was a flying bird. It provides no clues as to how this important difference between reptiles and birds might have evolved.

What about the wing claws? They are actually less reptile-like than those found on some living birds. The familiar ostrich has wing claws, as well as the hoatzin of South America and the touraco of Africa. There are also living, flightless birds with very small breastbones. No living adult birds have teeth, but several fossil birds had teeth, and many reptiles do not have teeth. It seems that teeth are not much help in telling the two groups apart. No living bird has a bony tail; but then each different kind of bird has some special feature or features that set it off from all other kinds of birds.

It would seem that an evolutionary link should possess in-between traits of various kinds. Whales have a mixture of fish traits and mammal traits, yet no one regards these as a link showing how fish evolved into mammals, or vice versa. What about *Archaeopteryx*? Is it an odd mixture, or does it give us real clues as to how certain traits might have evolved?

Hoatzin Touraco Ostrich

Figure 2.30 *Three living birds with wing claws like those of Archaeopteryx.*

Figure 2.31 *National Geographic writes of the transition from hairy, four-legged mammals to whales. Whales are mammals with some fish-like traits (see Dec. 1976, National Geographic insert).*

Figure 2.32 *Supposed transitions from reptile to bird. What kinds of problems would these hypothetical creatures face? (After Ostrom, J.H., "Bird Flight: How Did It Begin," American Scientist 67:46-56, 1979).*

Place in the column is also important from the evolutionary point of view. Since parental forms must come before their offspring, ancestors should be found lower in the fossil column. Recently, fossils of modern birds have been found in upper Jurassic rocks. This is the same system in which *Archaeopteryx* is found. Can *Archaeopteryx* be the ancestor of modern bird types if they existed side by side?

Figure 2.33 *Recently, bones of modern birds were reported from the same geologic system as those of Archaeopteryx.*

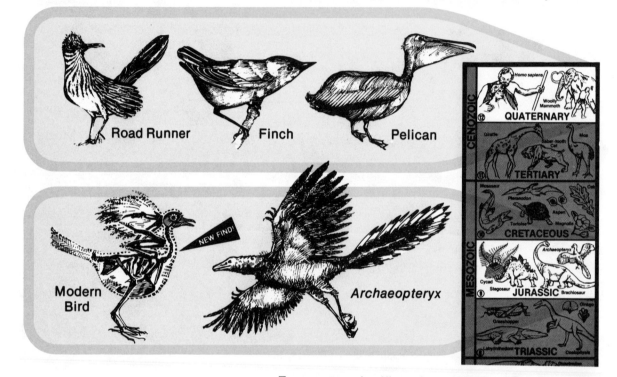

Even more significantly, recently, paleontologists have found fossils of a bird in Texas that they believe to be 75 million years older than *Archaeopteryx*. If this is true, and evolution has occurred, we would expect this bird to be much more reptile-like than *Archaeopteryx*, but just the opposite is true. In some respects, it is more bird-like than *Archaeopteryx*. For example, unlike most modern birds, which have a large bony keel, or sternum (the living hoatzin is one exception), *Archaeopteryx* apparently had a small keel, or sternum. The fossil bird, found in Texas, had a substantial bony keel, similar to modern birds. The Texas bird had hollow bones, like most modern birds, but *archaeopteryx* had solid bones (so do some modern birds). Thus, this fossil bird seems to have characteristics just opposite to that expected on the basis of evolution, and would seem

❝In spite of the fact that it is undeniably related to the two classes of reptiles and birds (a relation which the anatomy and physiology of actually living specimens demonstrates) we are not even authorized to consider the exceptional case of the *Archaeopteryx* as a true link. By link, we mean a necessary stage of transition between classes such as reptiles and birds, or between smaller groups. An animal displaying characteristics belonging to two different groups cannot be treated as a true link as long as the mechanisms of transition remain unknown.**❞8**

to rule out *archaeopteryx* as a transitional form between reptile and bird.

Can *Archaeopteryx* tell us anything about the origin of flight? Although experts do not agree as to whether its wings were used for gliding or flying, all agree that *Archaeopteryx* had true wings. No fossils, that are partly legs and partly wings, have been found, as yet.

Many claim that *Archaeopteryx* does fit as a true in-between form. Others, while they believe birds have evolved from reptiles, are not so sure that *Archaeopteryx* qualifies as a link. Lecomte du Nouy, an expert in this field, does not feel that this fossil can be a link. He says there is just not enough scientific evidence.

Discussing possible links between basic kinds, in another place, Stephen Jay Gould and Niles Eldredge write that "curious mosaics like *Archaeopteryx* do not count."[9] Another scientist, W. E. Swinton, an expert on birds, also indicates strong doubts about the fossil as an in-between form.

Let's review the basics: It seems that *Archaeopteryx* may not tell us much about the origin of feathers or the origin of flight. However, what about its strange combination of bird-like and reptile-like traits? Does *Archaeopteryx* qualify as an evolutionary link between reptiles and birds? Creationist scientists claim that *Archaeopteryx* was a distinct kind of bird, and not a transitional form. What do you think?

"In spite of the fact that it is undeniably related to the two classes of reptiles and birds (a relation which the anatomy and physiology of actually living specimens demonstrates) we are not even authorized to consider the exceptional case of the *Archaeopteryx* as a true link. By link, we mean a necessary stage of transition between classes such as reptiles and birds, or between smaller groups. An animal displaying characteristics belonging to two different groups cannot be treated as a true link as long as the mechanisms of transition remain unknown."[8]

"The origin of birds is largely a matter of deduction. There is no fossil evidence of the stages through which the remarkable change from reptile to bird was achieved."[10]

INTERPRET THE DATA

1. What would an evolutionist expect to find as evidence of change from reptiles to birds?

2. What features of *Archaeopteryx* make it a possible connecting link between reptiles and birds? List them.

3. What features of *Archaeopteryx* make creationists feel this is a distinct kind of bird?

4. What does *Archaeopteryx* tell us about the origin of feathers? . . . of flight?

5. How do creationists view the evidence of modern birds recently found in Jurassic rock along with *Archaeopteryx*? What does this evidence mean to evolutionists? What about the fossil bird found in Texas?

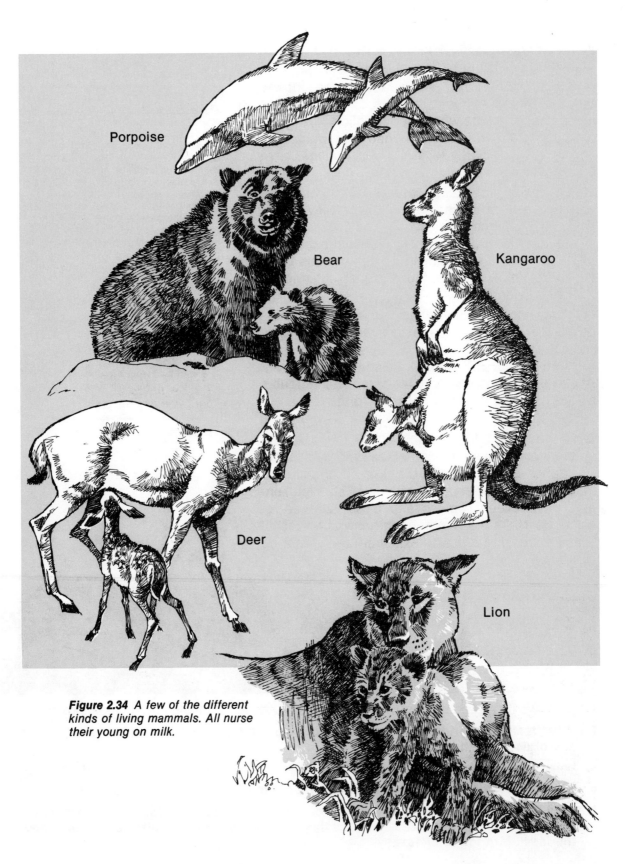

Porpoise

Bear

Kangaroo

Deer

Lion

Figure 2.34 *A few of the different kinds of living mammals. All nurse their young on milk.*

Origin of Mammals

Mammals are hairy, warm-blooded animals that give milk, such as cats, dogs, rabbits, deer, bears, and many other familiar creatures.

The mammals are almost missing from lower systems in the column series. However, there is a bursting forth of many mammal types in the lower Tertiary system. Running forms, swimming forms, and flying forms all appear suddenly and at the same time. The "first" fossil bat, one of the most highly specialized mammals, appears in the lowest Tertiary strata. Figure 2.35 shows a fossil which looks like a bat you would find today. In-between forms are not found. One other highly specialized group, the whales, also appears in the mammalian "explosion" without links to any other group. In fact, all 32 orders of mammals occur as distinct groups from their "first" appearance in the column. This is similar to the seeming "explosion" of many flowering plants in the Cretaceous and marine life in the Cambrian.

Figure 2.35 *The outline of a modern bat easily fits over the bones of the "first" fossil bat. (After Jepsen, G.L.)*

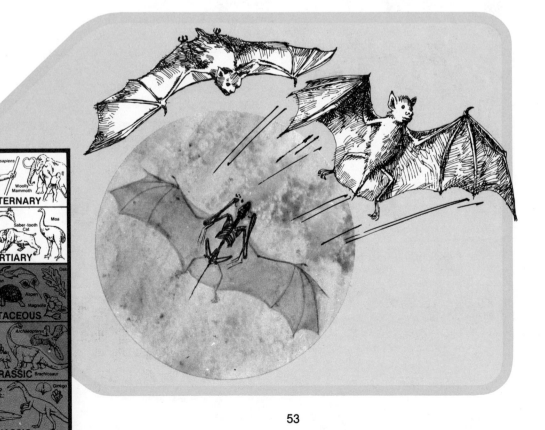

Mammal-like reptiles are also found as fossils. Many claim that these show how mammals may have evolved from reptiles (Figure 2.36).

Mammal-like reptiles occur almost as low in the column as reptiles themselves (see Figure 2.21, p. 41). Their running position seems to have been more like that of mammals than reptiles. In some, the jawbones are reduced in number and are smaller compared to those of ordinary reptiles. It has been suggested that the way the jaw is hinged to the skull is part reptile and part mammal. Some researchers believe that two of the jawbones moved up into the ear (Figure 2.37). How would hearing and chewing have been affected while the reptile was changing to a mammal?

All mammals, whether living or fossil, have three earbones and a single bone in the lower jaw. All reptiles, living or fossil, have a single earbone, and at least four bones in the lower jaw. There are no in-between forms.

Bones are not really the big difference between mammals and reptiles anyway.[11] Reptile babies develop inside egg shells apart from their mother. Mammal babies develop attached to their mother, and depend on her blood flow for life. There are fossils of reptiles inside their eggs, but no fossils, of course, of mammal babies inside their mothers. There is no generally accepted idea of how such a change could have occurred.

Egg-laying mammals, like the platypus, do not seem to be of any help in this matter. These

Figure 2.36 *The mammal-like reptiles (therapsids) had a higher walking stance than other reptiles.*

Figure 2.37 *The inferred transition of reptile jawbones into mammal earbones.*

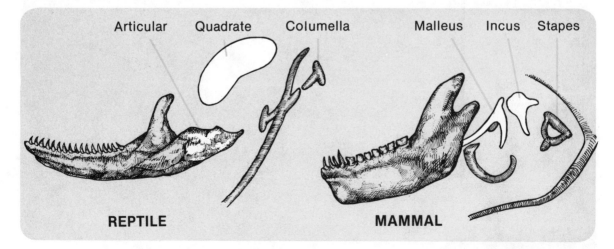

Articular   Quadrate   Columella   Malleus   Incus   Stapes

REPTILE   MAMMAL

54

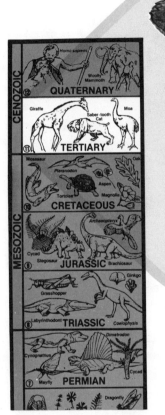

Figure 2.38 *The winsome platypus has a curious mixture of traits. It lays eggs like a reptile, but has fur and gives milk like a mammal. It uses echo location like some bats and dolphins. Is it a created mosaic of complete traits, or an animal caught in an in-between stage of evolution?*

Australian creatures (Figure 2.38) have hair and nourish their young on milk, like mammals. However, their young hatch from eggs as reptiles do. They also have duck-like bills and webbed feet. Few argue that these are the links between reptiles and mammals. Neither are they said to be bird and mammal links. There seem to be several reasons for this: 1. The egg structures and milk glands of these creatures are fully developed. They offer no clue as to the origin of the womb or the milk glands; 2. Platypus fossils look just like forms living today; 3. "Regular" mammals are found much lower in the column than the egg-laying platypus. Some argue that the platypus is a distinct kind, a mosaic or mixture of complete traits. These traits are found both in living forms and among fossils.

There is one mammal, however, which is often offered as proof that traits can evolve beyond the original kind. That mammal is the horse.

Figure 2.39 *Reptile babies develop inside eggshells, but mammal babies develop in the womb and are nourished by their mothers. Can you imagine how changes from reptile-egg to mammal-womb might have occurred?*

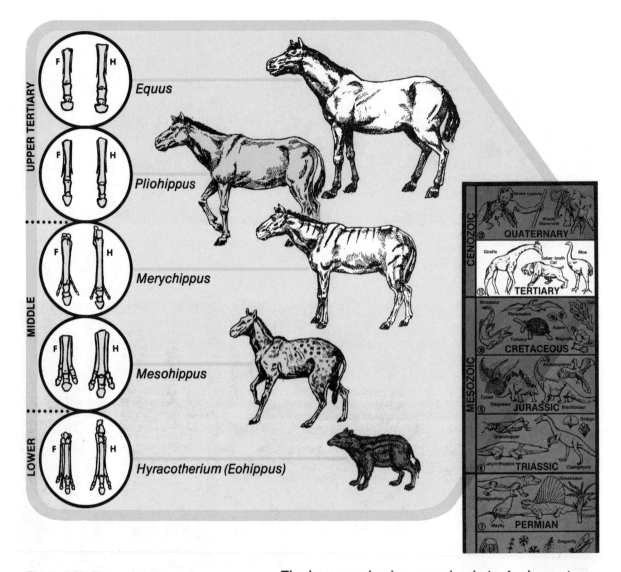

The series above shows a

Figure 2.40 *The series above shows a reduction in the number of hoofed toes, an increase in size, and lengthening of the face, all leading up to the features of the modern horse. Are there any valid objections to calling this an excellent evolutionary series? (F = Foreleg; H = Hindleg)*

The horse series is second only to *Archaeopteryx* as the most popular fossil evidence cited in support of evolution. Some say the horse series may be even better than *Archaeopteryx.* It is possible, unlike *Archaeopteryx,* to arrange the fossil specimens to show a series of changes.

The story of horse evolution as it is usually told in textbooks is pictured in Figure 2.40. The story starts in lower Tertiary rock with the dawn horse (*Eohippus* or *Hyracotherium),* a terrier-sized animal with a short snout, browsing teeth, and several toes (three rear and four front). In middle Tertiary rocks there are larger animals with longer snouts and fewer toes, as shown.

Finally, we have the large, modern horse, *Equus*, with a long snout, tooth gap, and grazing teeth. It has only one toe bone, with small, bordering splint bones. Some feel that these were left as remains of the other toes in its ancestors.

Leading evolutionists have criticized the horse story as it is often told. Scientists having studied horses, point out that teeth are either browsing or grazing types, never in-between. Size and snout length vary greatly within kind, as different breeds of dogs show. Argentine horse breeder, Fallabella, has selectively bred horses over just a few years to produce "house pet horses" only 17 inches tall.

Figure 2.41 Both horses here are mature adults! Can you think of other examples of great variation within a group of plants or animals?

There is also change in toe number. However, three and one-toed horses are found together in middle Tertiary rock. No transition between the three-toed and single-toed horse has been found. Creationists think that, rather than showing a gradual series, these fossils show different creatures living at the same time, just as we find monkeys, apes, and men in the fossil record. They state that different kinds of antelopes, zebras, elands, gnus, and gazelles could also be arranged in a series. In spite of this, they are distinctly different animals. Lecomte du Nouy in *Human Destiny* says that each stage of horse development appears suddenly, with no in-between forms. This statement by du Nouy tells us clearly that there are serious gaps in the horse series. He states that, while he thinks the in-between forms existed, they have not yet been found.

"But each one of these intermediaries seems to have appeared 'suddenly' and it has not yet been possible, because of the lack of fossils, to reconstruct the passage between these intermediaries. Yet it must have existed. The known forms remain separated like the piers of a ruined bridge. We know that the bridge has been built, but only vestiges of the stable props remain. The continuity we surmise may never be established by facts!"[8]

Eland   Gnu   Bushbuck   Gazelle   Dik-dik

Figure 2.42 *Although the animals above form a series, it is not an evolutionary series. Why not?*

Recently (1979), paleontologist David Raup included the horse among the "classic cases" of evolution that "have had to be discarded or modified as the result of more detailed information."[12]

The so-called five-toed horses may have nothing to do with horses at all. Actually, the original bones were named *Hyracotherium* because they looked like a hyrax (a rock badger or coney). It was pictured in museums and textbooks as a horse, even when there was not a single mounted skeleton of this animal in existence. The story of horse evolution seems clear enough in museums and textbook pictures. But what about the fossils themselves? Horses are thought to be the best or next best evidence of evolution. Examine the evidence. Where does it lead you?

EXAMINE THE DATA

1. How is the "horse series" used to support evolution?

2. State the criticisms by both creationists and evolutionists of the horse story.

3. Does the horse series give better support to evolution than *Archaeopteryx*? Explain your view.

4. What does the weight of fossil evidence seem to tell us about the origin of animals?

5. What *can't* the fossil evidence tell us about a once living form? List some examples. Why is this important in a study of the origin of mammals?

6. How does a creationist understand the great variety of mammals in lower Tertiary rock? How would an evolutionist respond?

Summary of Fossil Kinds

We have briefly examined fossils from all the major groups of living things — invertebrates, plants, and vertebrates. (The origin of man will be studied in a separate module.) We have pointed out known gaps between the groups we find as fossils. We have also looked at possible evolutionary connecting links, such as Archaeopteryx and the horse series. Scientists agree that the gaps are real and the differences are strong.

In 1859 Darwin wrote that lack of in-between forms as fossils was "perhaps the most serious objection to the theory [of evolution]." He thought the "missing links" would be found. Scientists have now worked with millions of tons of fossils for over 120 years. Well-known paleontologists David Raup and David Kitts say the gaps are still there.

> "Well, we are now about 120 years after Darwin and, . . . ironically, we have even fewer examples of evolutionary transition than we had in Darwin's time. By this I mean that some of the classic cases of Darwinian change in the fossil record, such as the evolution of the horse in North America, have had to be discarded or modified as the result of more detailed information." [12]

> "Despite the bright promise that paleontology provides a means of 'seeing' evolution, it has presented some nasty difficulties for evolutionists, the most notorious of which is the presence of 'gaps' in the fossil record. Evolution requires intermediate forms between species and paleontology does not provide them." [13]

Not many scientists are giving up the idea of evolution, but some are changing the theory a great deal. In 1952, Richard B. Goldschmidt said that a reptile once laid an egg, and the first bird hatched from that reptile egg. He called these sudden new forms "hopeful monsters." Many laughed at Goldschmidt for saying that. Scientists point out that hopeful monsters have never been observed; they probably could not find a mate anyway. But today, some paleontologists, led by S. J. Gould, are suggesting "the return of hopeful monsters."[14]

Gould and Niles Eldredge state that fossils, like living forms, vary only mildly around the average or "equilibrium" for each kind. But, they say, the sudden appearance of a species can interrupt or "punctuate" this equilibrium. According to this new concept of **"punctuated equilibrium,"** fossils are not supposed to show in-between forms between species. The new forms appeared suddenly, in large steps.

punctuated equilibrium: the idea that evolution occurs in large steps in small populations, a new idea used by a few evolutionists to explain the lack of in-between forms as fossils

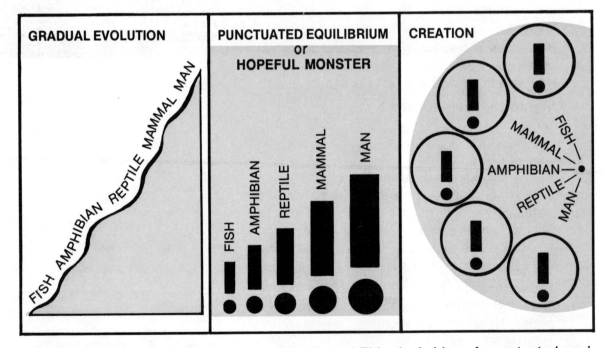

Figure 2.43 Followers of the punctuated equilibrium idea agree with creationists that fossils show only limited variation within separate kinds. They attempt to explain these observations by offering a new evolutionary model. What is their view? Compare it to creation.

Gould's and Eldredge's idea of punctuated equilibrium is based on the fossils that are not found. They believe that a given kind of life did gradually evolve, but they argue that the changes were in sudden leaps, and left no fossil evidence. They agree that the fossil record is one of orderly gaps.

They are trying to change evolutionary thinking to fit these observed gaps. However, these gaps in the fossil record are predicted by creationists. Except for extinction, creationists expect to find, as fossils, only varieties of existing kinds, separated into distinct groups such as we have today. Furthermore, the idea of punctuated equilibrium is designed to explain only the gaps between species, not big gaps, such as those between invertebrates and fish. The big mysteries would remain unexplained, even if the idea of punctuated equilibrium is true.

What does the fossil evidence itself say? Well, fossils cannot speak for themselves. It is not a matter of one fossil here or there, it is the total amount of evidence. Which model do the facts fit best?

What do you think? Are you willing to search and compare all of the data?

STOP REVIEW THE DATA

1. What are "hopeful monsters?" How do they fit into the idea of evolution?

2. Why do some evolutionists propose the ideas of "hopeful monsters" and *punctuated equilibrium* in place of older concepts of evolution? How do other evolutionists and creationists respond?

3. Even if no in-between forms are found, some evolutionists argue that the geologic column itself shows evolution. Sea organisms are at the bottom and land plants farther up. Among the vertebrates, fish are lowest, then amphibians and reptiles, and finally mammals and birds. How do creationists interpret this sequence?

4. The next chapter reviews all the fossil evidence—first, as an evolutionist, then as a creationist sees it. What evidence do you think the evolutionist will hit hardest?...the creationist?

Figure 3.1 *Let us see how well you can put the pieces of the fossil puzzle together. How well do your assumptions fit the facts?*

CHAPTER THREE

Putting It All Together

We have looked at a lot of data about fossils and about the rocks in which they are found. We have looked at this data from two different points of view: the **creation** model and the **evolution** model. Which of these models seems to fit best? Where are the strong and weak points? Where is the evidence incomplete?

It is hard to approach these questions without our feelings becoming involved. When we dig into the history of life, we cannot help but wonder how we ourselves came into being. We wonder about our purpose and destiny. Our questions become more difficult when we find much of the data are only *circumstantial.* That is, these data are subject to more than one interpretation. No human observed the beginning of life, and we cannot test what happened in the past. We cannot even be sure how helpful present methods are in explaining past events. In short, if there is a subject that needs an open mind, the study of fossils is that subject.

For these reasons we have taken a two-model approach in our discussion of the fossil evidence. By looking at a broad range of data in the light of two contrasting ideas, we hope we have stirred you to think for yourself. We hope you will notice where **fact** and **assumption** lie. Finally, we hope you will be considerate of ideas different from yours.

To help you put your own ideas together, let us review the fossil data: first, as an evolutionist would put it together and, then, as a creationist sees it. If you were listening to two such men speaking at a conference, what *assumptions* would each be making? What are the areas where further research is needed? Can either case be established beyond a reasonable doubt? Which seems to offer the best promise for further research? What do *you* think?

evolution: *(ev-o-'loo-shun)* the idea that offspring of simple life forms can change into varied and more complex kinds over long periods of time; change *between* kinds

creation: *(cree-'a-shun)* the idea that all life forms are varieties of kinds created by a Master Designer; change *within* kinds

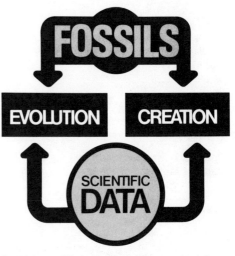

fact: something observed or measured

assumption: an unprovable belief used as a basis for reasoning

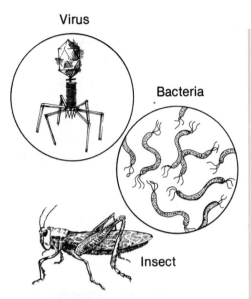

Virus

Bacteria

Insect

Figure 3.2 *Many changes in heredity ("mutations") have been observed in viruses, bacteria and insects.*

*For discussion of these points, see other modules in this series (General Resource Books, p.79).

Figure 3.3 *Only fossils of sea life are found at the base of the geologic column.*

EVOLUTIONIST SUMMATION

Life began in the oceans over 3 billion years ago. Although we may never be able to work out all the details, it seems that only time, chance, and natural processes were involved. Science cannot deal with a God. Once life began, variation and natural selection took place. This insured an increase in complex and diverse forms of life. We see mutations taking place about us everyday. Flu viruses change, insects become resistant to DDT, and bacteria learn to live on penicillin. These are only a few of the many things that show evolution in action.*

The fossil record is silent concerning *evolutionary* changes that must have occurred during life's first 2½ billion years. However, about 600 million years ago, in Cambrian times, many animal groups developed hard parts at about the same time, and these left many fossils. These fossils help us trace the changes of life upward through the geologic column.*

The Cambrian rocks show life began in the sea. It was not until about 200 million years later that we find evidence of land plants and animals. Flowering plants did not appear until the Cretaceous. This was the last of the three periods in the "Age of

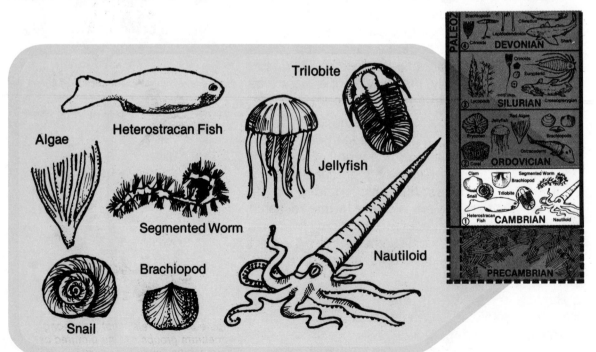

Algae

Heterostracan Fish

Segmented Worm

Trilobite

Jellyfish

Snail

Brachiopod

Nautiloid

Reptiles." The reptiles, including dinosaurs, ruled the earth for nearly 200 million years. Will man, who appeared perhaps only 2 – 4 million years ago, prove himself as able to survive?

Much of the past invertebrate fossil data is missing. For this reason, fossil history must be worked out by studying living forms. The search continues for the history of land plants, seed plants, and flowering plants. Their remains do not preserve as well as shells, bones, and teeth. On the other hand, the story of vertebrate evolution is clearly shown.

The first vertebrates, the fish, appear in upper Cambrian rock. Their change from invertebrates must have occurred in earlier times (lower Cambrian or Precambrian). A comparison of the remains of lobe-finned fishes with those of certain amphibians (Figure 3.5) helps us picture the change from water to land.

Figure 3.4 Plants found as fossils.

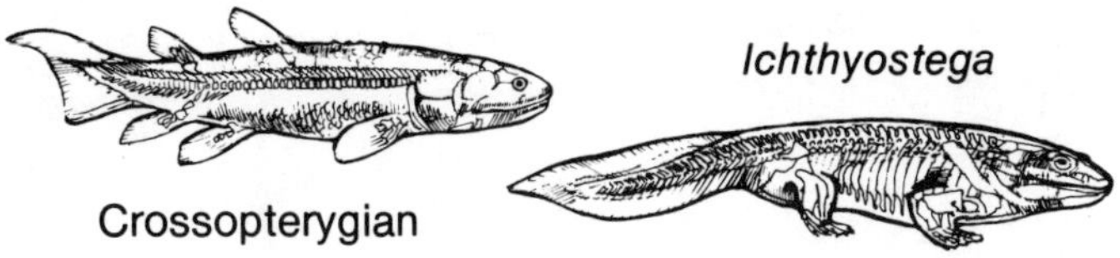

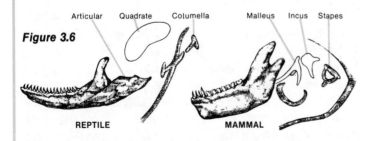

Ichthyostega

Crossopterygian

Figure 3.5 There are many similarities in the bones of crossopterygian fish and amphibians like Ichthyostega.

When some amphibians gave up the last traces of water existence (their tadpole stage), they then changed into reptiles. Some reptiles almost immediately evolved into mammal-like forms. A series of fossil forms shows the evolution of mammal earbones from reptile jawbones (Figure 3.6).

Figure 3.6

Articular   Quadrate   Columella   Malleus   Incus   Stapes

REPTILE   MAMMAL

But the most striking example of evolutionary change is provided by the famous "reptile-bird," *Archaeopteryx*. *Archaeopteryx* is truly an in-between link. It has feathers and a bird-like beak;

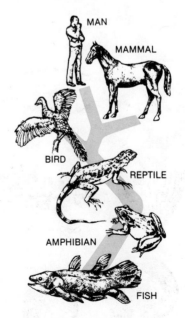

MAN

MAMMAL

BIRD

REPTILE

AMPHIBIAN

FISH

Figure 3.7 The relationships among vertebrate groups can be pictured as a branching "evolutionary tree."

but it has teeth in its bill, wing claws, and a long, bony reptile-like tail. When little was known of the fossil record, Darwin complained that a lack of intermediate links was perhaps the most obvious and serious objection to evolution. Today, forms like *Archaeopteryx* are helping to fill those gaps. "The horse series," showing how a small, browsing animal changed into our modern horse, is also a good example (Figure 3.9).

Figure 3.8 *Archaeopteryx has features of both reptiles and birds, so it seems to be an evolutionary link between the two groups.*

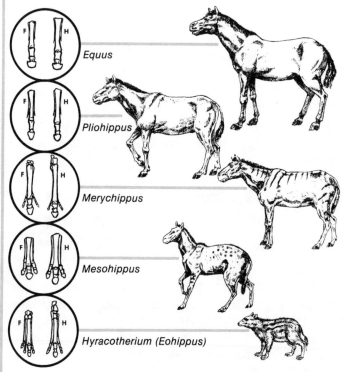

Equus

Pliohippus

Merychippus

Mesohippus

Hyracotherium (Eohippus)

Figure 3.9 *The "horse series."*

Of course, the best record of *evolutionary* change is the *geologic column* itself. Many parts of the column are exposed in the American Southwest. A walk through the canyons of Arizona and Utah is like a walk through the history of life. The base of Grand Canyon is Precambrian, with few fossil remains. But then comes Cambrian life, the sea creatures with which abundant life began. Walking up through the Paleozoic strata, we see the *trilobites* flourish. They die out, and the *lampshells* also largely give way to the *clams*. The *nautiloids* then change into *ammonites*. Near the top we find tracks of early land animals in the desert sands of

Permian times. In Utah to the north is the record of the dinosaur's reign. The beginnings of birds and mammals are also there. But for man's ancestry, we must go to Africa.

The fossil record of man is still not complete, but we are beginning to fill in the gaps there, too. As we search for our own past, we learn more about ourselves, our instincts, and ambitions. Perhaps we will even discover our reason for being and what the future holds. Some say over 90% of all known species have become extinct. Will man be able to beat the odds?

Figure 3.10 *A walk from the base to the top of Grand Canyon would take you through nearly half the systems in the geologic column, and you would see only one gap.*

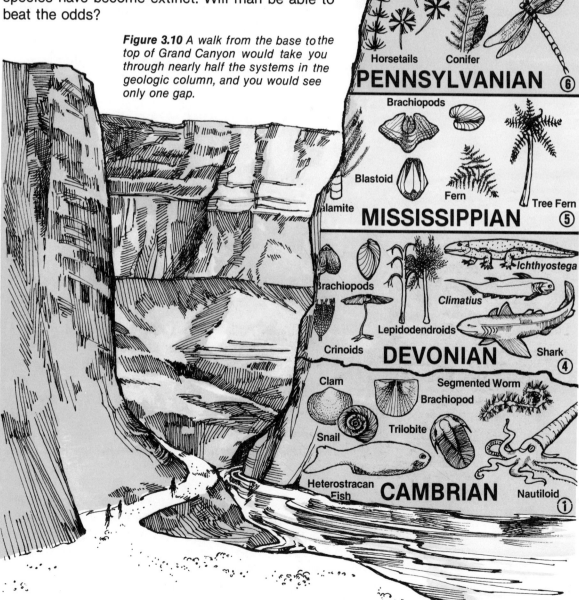

PERMIAN ⑦
Cycad

PENNSYLVANIAN ⑥
Dragonfly
Horsetails Conifer

MISSISSIPPIAN ⑤
Brachiopods
Blastoid
Fern
Tree Fern
Calamite

DEVONIAN ④
Ichthyostega
Climatius
Shark
Brachiopods
Lepidodendroids
Crinoids

CAMBRIAN ①
Clam
Segmented Worm
Brachiopod
Snail
Trilobite
Heterostracan Fish
Nautiloid

The evolutionist suggests a picture of the history of life on earth. Before we look at the creationist summation, review the data in your own mind.

REVIEW THE CASE

1. **What is the strongest factual evidence the evolutionist offers to support his case?**
2. **What key assumptions does the speaker make?**
3. **What are the weakest points in the speaker's case?**

CREATIONIST SUMMATION

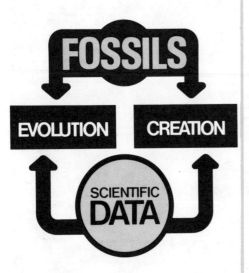

We can easily tell the difference between a hand-sculptured marble statue and a desert sandstone formation carved by the natural processes of weathering and erosion. When scientists study the smallest details of life, they find a special type of order that exists only in created objects. The molecules within them show the kind of relationships possible only in created objects. We also observe that living things multiply only after their *kind* with limited difference. It takes engineering analysis, a principle of creation, to understand the marvelous fit of organisms to their environment. Many scientists openly wonder and challenge others to think whether the *kind* of design seen in living things does imply a Designer. Clearly creation seems to be the best idea from our present knowledge of cells, heredity, and ecology. Our observations of fossils, the best historical evidence, strongly supports the creation model. Creationists look for symmetry (order), purpose (a reason to be), and interdependence (all parts working for the benefit of the whole system). This is precisely what we see in the real living world.

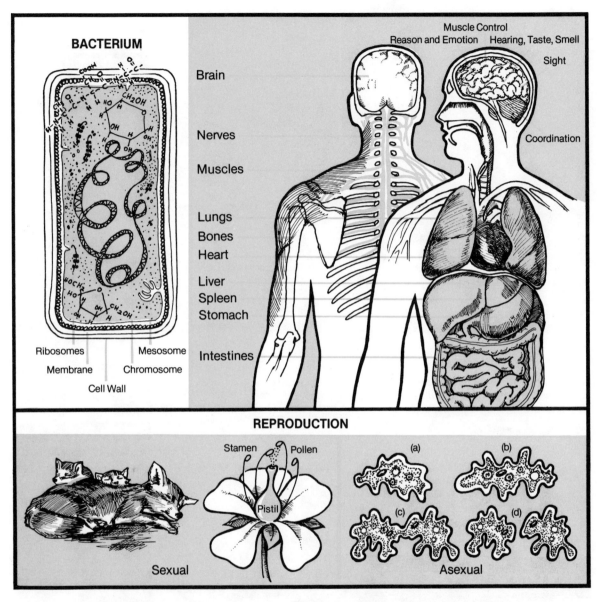

BACTERIUM

Ribosomes
Membrane
Cell Wall
Mesosome
Chromosome

Brain

Nerves

Muscles

Lungs
Bones
Heart

Liver
Spleen
Stomach

Intestines

Reason and Emotion
Muscle Control
Hearing, Taste, Smell
Sight
Coordination

REPRODUCTION

Stamen
Pollen
Pistil

Sexual

(a) (b) (c) (d)

Asexual

Figure 3.11 *Living things have many features of design that point back to origin by creation.*

Figure 3.12 *Both formations look like a man's head, but (b) was cut by weathering and erosion, while (a) must have been purposefully hand-crafted or created. We can also infer creation from our observations of living things.*

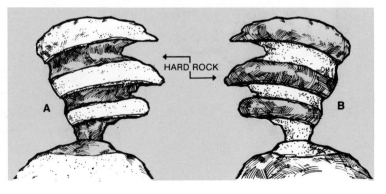

HARD ROCK

A

B

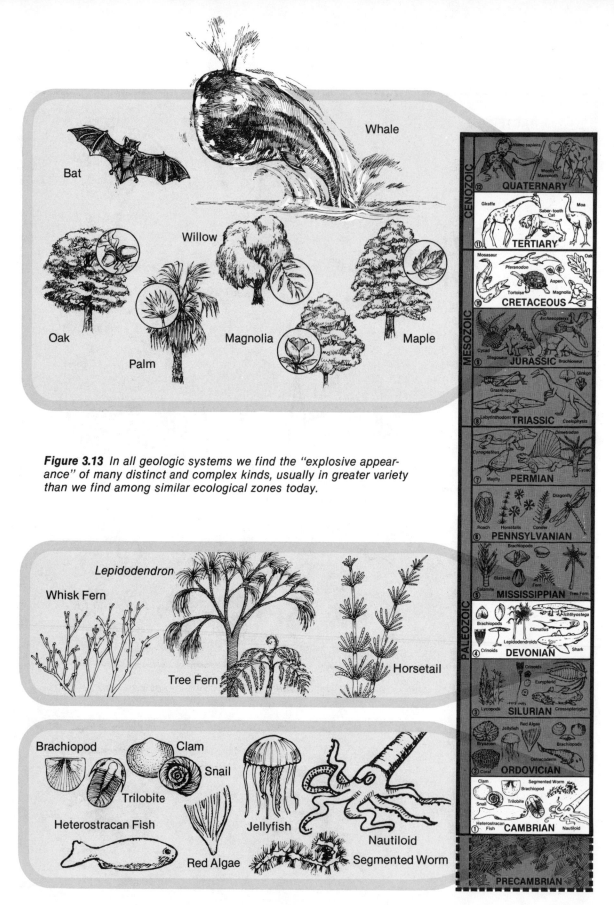

Figure 3.13 *In all geologic systems we find the "explosive appear-ance" of many distinct and complex kinds, usually in greater variety than we find among similar ecological zones today.*

70

When we find *invertebrate* fossils, we find complete clams, snails, jellyfish, sponges, trilobites, etc. All of these kinds are separate and distinct at their *first* appearance in Cambrian deposits. Among the Cambrian *invertebrates* we find the *squid-like nautiloids.* These have the *most complex* overall design of all the sea creatures. Their eyes are nearly as intricate as ours. Perhaps even more complex are the fantastic compound eyes of the trilobites. These are highly adapted organisms that have now become extinct. Nowhere on the earth can we find ancestors for these complex animals. Neither can we find in-between forms linking them to each other.

Change within *kind* is also the rule for plant groups. All the major groups of *algae* are present as distinct kinds in Cambrian rocks. The ferns and fern allies appear as distinct and diverse kinds in the Devonian. Flowering plants appear suddenly and at the same time in such familiar forms as oak, willow, and magnolia in dinosaur strata. As botanist E.J.H. Corner of Cambridge University summarized it, ". . . to the unprejudiced, the fossil record of plants is in favor of special creation."

The same is true of vertebrate fossils. All 32 orders of mammals appear as distinct groups in lower Tertiary rock. The most highly specialized, the flying bats and swimming whales, appear at the beginning of the mammal explosion as fully developed and separate kinds.

The first fish found as fossils are clearly fish. They are distinct and very special groups. Fossils of regular birds appear in the same strata as that odd bird, *Archaeopteryx*. *Archaeopteryx* has teeth similar to a few fossil birds and wing claws like only a few living birds. However, *Archaeopteryx* has complex feathers of several different kinds. These facts suggest that feathers and flight were designed by special creation.

The fossils also clearly show that man has always been man. Skeleton's of modern man occasionally have been discovered in rock dated by evolutionists as lower Tertiary, much older than man's supposed ape-like ancestors.

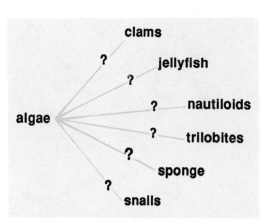

Figure 3.14 Complex marine invertebrates are found in Cambium deposits looking much the same as they do today (except for those like the trilobites, which have become extinct). No intermediate forms between these invertebrates and their supposed single-cell ancestors have ever been found.

Figure 3.15 Archaeopteryx has well developed feathers and wings and is found no deeper in the column than "regular" birds, so it seems to be a distinct created kind.

Perhaps the biggest mystery concerning fossils is why so many *adapted* forms of life, especially giants, become extinct. There is much observable and historical evidence to suggest that the earth was once covered by the waters of a global flood.

Figure 3.16 *According to the creation-catastrophe model, the geologic column represents the usual series in which different flood sediments rose progressively from ocean depths to upland environments.*

Figure 3.17 *Some creationists suggest that geologic systems are the fossil remains of plants and animals once living at the same time in different ecological zones.*

Flood conditions are ideal for forming fossils. Such a flood would help us to explain extinction and also much of what we observe about fossil deposits.

Groups of fossils suggest that the rising flood waters buried different *ecological zones.* The usual sequence of burial is shown by the *geologic column.* Life from all ecological zones lived at the same time, however, causing the ideal geologic column to be regularly interrupted by "misplaced" fossils and by gaps in the sequence.

Even some evolutionists (who call themselves **"neo-catastrophists"**) admit there is much evidence for massive flooding of the continents. This evidence includes **polystratic** fossils that cut across many *sedimentary* layers; huge fossil graveyards with billions of specimens; and the great deposits of water-laid coal seams stretching across half of North America. All of these show broad and rapid processes of sedimentation. This, of course, is completely unlike anything we see going on today, but it can be *inferred* from our observations of sedimentary rocks.

The evidence for creation and variation is clear enough from the fossil evidence. However, much work needs to be done to refine the flood model.

Figure 3.18 *"Fossil graveyards," like that in Agate Springs, Nebraska, suggest a major catastrophe trapped many animals under a heavy sediment load.*

neo-catastrophists: evolutionists who, like many creationists, use major flooding to help explain fossil deposits and extinction

polystratic: fossils that span many layers of rocks

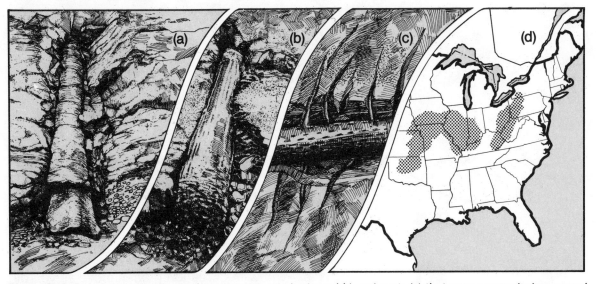

Figure 3.19 *Polystratic fossils, such as the tree trunks (a and b), and roots (c) that span many strata suggest that great depths of sediment were laid down rapidly. Many polystrates are found in coal deposits that cover broad areas (d), and some evolutionists, called "neo-catastrophists," agree with creationists that these suggest massive flooding of the continents.*

Such work, in fact, is being done—by experiments on coal, cave formation, oil well pressure, pollen distribution, animal tracks in sediment, and many others. The final answers are not all in yet, but the promise of fruitful research is truly exciting. Several problems in early creation models have already been solved, and further research promises to strengthen the model.

But the evidence for creation does not come from creationists. It comes from nature, from fossils, and from the world of living things. By logic and observation, we can tell the difference between objects produced by time and chance and those produced by creative design. Without seeing either the creator or the creative act, for example, we can recognize a pottery fragment as the product of human creation. That same scientific skill allows us to recognize evidence of creation, even when the Creator must be far greater than human minds can understand. As we study the handiwork of the Master Designer, we may also learn something about our relationship to the Creator of all life on earth — a mind-stretching idea that gives our lives and our science deeper and richer meaning.

Figure 3.20 *The creation model has stimulated research on animals' tracks made under water (a); fossil land plant spores in Cambrian rock (b); and rapid formation of cave features, which include a bat encased in dripstone (c).*

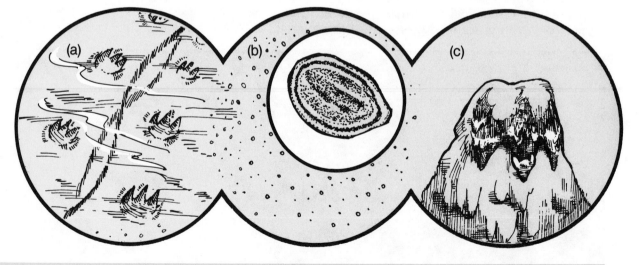

You have now heard the summaries for both cases. Review the creation model above as you did the evolution model earlier. Then use the questions on the next page to compare the two models. Which model fits the best? What do *you* think and why?

1. How would a *creationist* view the invertebrate fossil evidence? The plant fossils?

2. How would an *evolutionist* view the invertebrate fossil evidence? The plant fossils?

3. How do *evolutionists* interpret *Archaeopteryx*? The horse series?

4. How do *creationists* interpret *Archaeopteryx*? The horse series?

5. What do *evolutionists* say about the vertebrate fossil finds and in-between forms? What do *creationists* say?

6. Interpret the geologic column from an *evolutionist's* point of view.

7. Interpret the geologic column from a *creationist's* point of view.

8. Make a chart showing what you consider the strongest and weakest points of the creation and evolution models.

9. List the points in both the evolution model and the creation model that go beyond the facts and require faith.

10. Can the case for either evolution or creation be established "beyond a reasonable doubt"?

11. Do you think a two-model approach was profitable? Was there enough data on both sides to challenge you? Was this module on fossils fairly presented?

12. Did the two-model approach help you develop skill in scientific reasoning? Did it help you to understand and appreciate the opinions of people with different ideas?

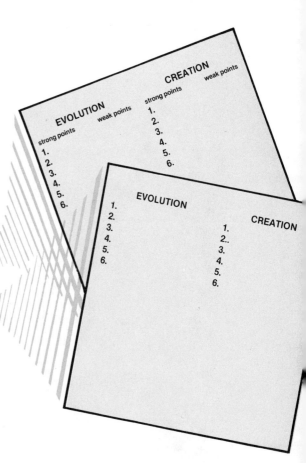

CONCLUSION

One of the most important parts of a study, such as this, is how you have drawn your conclusions. All too often students have been trained to agree with the thoughts of others. Now, in this module, two opposing ideas have been stated on a subject for you to ponder. You have been asked to become a **decision-maker,** a person who can think for himself. In this process you have learned to test your own ideas and those of others, even ideas presented in books, news, and the classroom. As you made up your mind, you should have learned to use the "process skills" of science. These skills not only help you make decisions about scientific data, but life as well.

decision-maker: someone who is able to examine data objectively and make clear judgments

---

PROCESS SKILLS

1. **Observation** (sight, hearing, smell, etc.)
2. **Classification** (placing information in categories)
3. **Inferring** (general assumptions about data)
4. **Predicting** (always done from considerable data)
5. **Measuring** (using standards for measurement)
6. **Communicating** (oral, written charts, graphs, etc.)
7. **Interpreting Data** (from all aspects of the investigation: classifying, communicating, inferring, etc.)
8. **Making Operational Definitions** (definitions that are clear and expressive of the process)
9. **Formulating Questions and Hypothesis** (a sophisticated stage, including all presently known data)
10. **Experimentation** (one of the best ways of making judgments relative to a problem. Empirical knowledge)
11. **Formulating Models** (models are temporary structures that quickly change when new information becomes available)

REFERENCES

1. **Axelrod, Daniel I.,** "Early Cambrian Marine Fauna," *Science, Vol. 128, 1958,* p. 7.

2. **Bold, Harold C.,** *Morphology of Plants,* 2nd ed., Harper & Row, New York, 1967.

3. **Corner, E.J.H.,** "Evolution," in Contemporary Botanical Thought, ed. by A.M. MacLeod and L.S. Cobley, Quadrangle Books, Chicago, 1961, p. 97.

4. **Romer, A.S.,** *Vertebrate Paleontology,* University of Chicago Press, Chicago, 1966.

5. **White, Errol,** "A Little on Lungfishes," *Proceedings of the Linnean Society of London,* Vol. 177, 1966, p. 8.

6. **Cox, Barry,** "Mysteries of Early Dinosaur Evolution," *Evolution,* Vol. 264, 1976, p. 314.

7. **Olson, E.C.** *The Evolution of Life,* The New American Library, New York, 1965, pp. 180-182.

8. **du Nouy, L.,** *Human Destiny,* The New American Library, New York, 1947, p. 74.

9. **Gould, S.J.** and **Eldredge, Niles,** "Punctuated Equilibria: The Tempo and Mode of Evolution Reconsidered," *Paleobiology,* Vol. 3, 1977, p. 147.

10. **Swinton, W.E.,** *Biology and Comparative Physiology of Birds,* A.J. Marshall, ed., Vol. 1, Academic Press, New York, 1960, p. 1.

11. **Valentine, J.W.,** "The Evolution of Multicellular Plants and Animals," *Scientific American,* Vol. 239, 1978, p. 157.

12. **Raup, David M.,** "Conflicts Between Darwin and Paleontology," *Field Museum of Natural History Bulletin,* Vol. 50, 1979, p. 25.

13. **Kitts, David,** "Paleontology and Evolutionary Theory," *Evolution,* Vol. 28, 1974, p. 467.

14. **Gould, Stephen Jay,** "The Return of Hopeful Monsters," *Natural History,* Vol. 86, June-July, 1977, pp. 22-30.

RESOURCE BOOKS

General Books

Bliss, Richard B. *Origins: Two Models, Evolution/Creation,* Creation-Life Publishers, San Diego, 1979.

Bliss, Richard B. and **Parker, Gary E.,** *Origin of Life* (Two Models), Creation-Life Publishers, San Diego, 1978.

*__Matthews, William III,__ *Fossils,* Barnes and Noble Books, New York, 1979.

Rhodes, Frank et al., *Fossils,* Golden Press, New York, 1979.

Evolution Books

Gastonguay, Paul R., *Evolution for Everyone* (Biological Sciences Curriculum Study), Bobbs-Merrill Co., Indianapolis, 1974.

Moore, Ruth, *Evolution,* Time-Life Books, New York, 1970.

*__Mayr, Ernst__ et al., *Evolution* (A Scientific American Book), W.H. Freeman and Company, San Francisco, 1978.

Thompson, W.R., Introduction to *Origin of Species,* Charles Darwin, Everyman's Library, E.P. Dutton & Co., New York, 1956.

Welch, Claude A. et al., *Molecules to Man* (Biological Sciences Curriculum Study), Houghton Mifflin Co., Boston, 1973.

Creation Books

Anderson, J. Kerby, *Fossils in Focus,* Zondervan Publishing Co., Grand Rapids, 1977.

Gish, Duane T., *Evolution: The Challenge of the Fossil Record,* Creation Life Publishers, San Diego, 1985.

*__Howe, George F.,__ ed., *Speak to the Earth,* Presbyterian & Reformed Pub. Co., Philadelphia, 1976.

Moore, John N. and **Slusher, Harold S.,** eds., *Biology: A Search for Order in Complexity,* Zondervan, Grand Rapids, 1977.

*__Morris, Henry M.__ ed., *Scientific Creationism,* Creation-Life Publishers, San Diego, 1978.

Morris, Henry M. and **Gary E. Parker,** *What Is Creation Science?,* Creation Life Publishers, San Diego, 1987.

*__Moore, John N.,__ *How to Teach Origins,* Mott Media, Milford, Mich. 1984.

*These books are written on a college reading level.

CREDITS

Designed by Marvin Ross, Art Director, Institute for Creation Research. Masthead cartoons on pages 25, 31, 34 by Marvin Ross. All other cartoons by Jonathan Chong. Cover, courtesy of ICR Museum of Creation and Earth History; photographs by Rex Salmon and Steve Pitman.

Figures 1.5, 1.6, 1.7, 1.11, 1.14, 1.15, 1.18, 2.4, 2.7, 2.8, 2.11, 2.15, 2.16, 2.17, 2.19, 2.23, 2.24, 2.26, 2.27, 2.28, 2.29, 2.32 (after Z. Burian, J.H. Ostrom), 2.38, 2.43, 3.4, 3.5, 3.8, 3.10 (with L. Sims), 3.11, 3.12, 3.16, 3.17—Marvin Ross.

Figures 1.8, 1.10, 2.1, 2.2, 2.9, 2.10, 2.20, 2.21, 2.22, 2.30, 2.31, 2.34, 2.36, 2.39, 2.40, 2.42, 3.1, 3.2, 3.9, 3.20—Jonathan Chong.

Figures 1.16, 1.17, 2.12, 2.13, 2.25, 2.35 (after G.L. Jepsen), 3.14—Marvin Ross, Jonathan Chong. Figures 2.14, 3.7, 3.19—Jay Wegter, Marvin Ross. Figure 2.33—Jay Wegter, Jonathan Chong, Marvin Ross. Figure 3.13—Jonathan Chong, Leslie Sims, Marvin Ross. Page vi, 3, 76—Marvin Ross, Jonathan Chong. Page 2—Leslie Sims. Page 3—Photograph by Steve Pitman.

Figure 1.1—Dinosaur National Monument. Figures 1.2, 1.3, 1.4, 2.6—ICR Museum of Creation and Earth History, Photographs by Steve Pitman, Paul Anderson. Figure 1.9—Photographs, courtesy of Dr. Leonard Brand, Loma Linda University. Figures 1.12, 2,3—Tim Ravenna, Jay Wegter. Figure 1.13—Cumberland Bone Cave. Figure 1.19—Tim Ravenna, Jay Wegter. Figures 2.5, 3.18—American Museum of Natural History. Figure 2.18—Jay Wegter. Figure 2.37, 3.6—Jay Wegter. Figure 2.41—Photograph, courtesy of UPI. Figure 3.3—Leslie Sims. Figure 3.15—Photograph, courtesy of John Morris.

Copy Editor—Charlotte Glasgow.